PRAISE FOR

# HOW TO WRITE A SENTENCE

"Both deeper and more democratic than *The Elements of Style*."
—*Financial Times*

"A guided tour through some of the most beautiful, arresting sentences in the English language." —*Slate*

"[Fish] shares his connoisseurship of the elegant sentence."
—*The New Yorker*

"Stanley Fish just might be America's most famous professor." —*BookPage*

"*How to Write a Sentence* is a compendium of syntactic gems—light reading for geeks." —*New York* magazine

"*How to Write a Sentence* isn't merely a prescriptive guide to the craft of writing but a rich and layered exploration of language as an evolving cultural organism. It belongs not on the shelf of your home library but in your brain's most deep-seated amphibian sensemaking underbelly."
—Maria Popova, *Brain Pickings*

"[Fish's] approach is genially experiential—a lifelong reader's engagement whose amatory enthusiasm is an attempt to overthrow Strunk & White's infamous insistences on grammar by rote." —*New York Observer*

"In this small feast of a book Stanley Fish displays his love of the English sentence. His connoisseurship is broad and deep, his examples are often breathtaking, and his analyses of how the masterpieces achieve their effects are acute and compelling." —*New Republic*

"A sentence is, in John Donne's words, 'a little world made cunningly,' writes Fish. He'll teach you the art." —*People* magazine

"This splendid little volume describes how the shape of a sentence controls its meaning." —*Boston Globe*

"Like a long periodic sentence, this book rumbles along, gathers steam, shifts gears, and packs a wallop."  —Roy Blount Jr.

"Language lovers will flock to this homage to great writing."  —*Booklist*

"Fish is a personable and insightful guide with wide-ranging erudition and a lack of pretension."  —*National Post*

"For both aspiring writer and eager reader, Fish's insights into sentence construction and care are instructional, even inspirational."  —*The Huffington Post*

"If you love language you'll find something interesting, if not fascinating, in [*How to Write a Sentence*]."  —CBSNews.com

"[A] slender but potent volume. Fish, a distinguished law professor and literary theorist, is the anti-Strunk & White."  —*Globe and Mail*

"You'd get your money's worth from the quotations alone. . . . If you give this book the attention it so clearly deserves, you will be well rewarded."  —*Washington Times*

"The fun comes from the examples cited throughout: John Updike, Jane Austen . . . all are cited throughout."  —*Washington Post*

"*How to Write a Sentence* is the first step on the journey to the Promised Land of good writing."  —*Saudi Gazette*

"*How to Write a Sentence* is a must-read for aspiring writers and anyone who wants to deepen their appreciation of literature. If extraordinary sentences are like sports plays, Fish is the Vin Scully of great writing."  —Gerald Graff and Cathy Birkenstein, authors of *They Say/I Say*

# HOW TO
# WRITE
*A*
# SENTENCE

Also by Stanley Fish

# HOW TO
# WRITE
# A
# SENTENCE

*and*

## HOW TO READ ONE

## STANLEY FISH

HARPER

NEW YORK • LONDON • TORONTO • SYDNEY

HARPER

Grateful acknowledgment is made for permission to reprint excerpts from the following:

"Permanently" from *The Collected Poems of Kenneth Koch* by Kenneth Koch, copyright © 2005 by The Kenneth Koch Literary Estate. Used by permission of Random House, Inc.

"Too Marvelous for Words," words by Johnny Mercer, music by Richard A. Whiting © 1937 (Renewed) WB Music Corp. All rights reserved. Used by permission.

A hardcover edition of this book was published in 2011 by HarperCollins Publishers.

HarperCollins books may be purchased for educational, business, or sales promotional use. For information please write: Special Markets Department, HarperCollins Publishers, 10 East 53rd Street, New York, NY 10022.

FIRST HARPER PAPERBACK PUBLISHED 2012.

*Designed by Emily Cavett Taff*

The Library of Congress has catalogued the hardcover edition of the book as follows:

Fish, Stanley Eugene.
     How to write a sentence : and how to read one / by Stanley
       Fish. — 1st ed.
       p. cm.
     ISBN 978-0-06-184054-8
     1. English language—Sentences. 2. English language—Grammar—Problems, exercises, etc. 3. English language—Rhetoric. I. Title.
     PE1441.F57 2011
     808'.042—dc22

                      2010033166

ISBN 978-0-06-184053-1 (pbk.)

To the Memory of Lucille Reilly Parry,
Teacher, 1911–2010

*One day the Nouns were clustered in the street.*
*An Adjective walked by, with her dark beauty.*
*The Nouns were struck, moved, changed.*
*The next day a Verb drove up, and created the Sentence.*

—Kenneth Koch, "Permanently"

*You're much too much, and just too very, very*
*To ever be in Webster's Dictionary*
*And so I'm borrowing a love song from the birds*
*To tell you that you're marvelous*
*Too marvelous for words.*

—Johnny Mercer, "Too Marvelous for Words"

# CONTENTS

# CHAPTER I

# WHY SENTENCES?

IN HER BOOK *The Writing Life* (1989), Annie Dillard tells the story of a fellow writer who was asked by a student, "Do you think I could be a writer?" "'Well,' the writer said, 'do you like sentences?'" The student is surprised by the question, but Dillard knows exactly what was meant. He was being told, she explains, that "if he liked sentences he could begin," and she remembers a similar conversation with a painter friend. "I asked him how he came to be a painter. He said, 'I like the smell of paint.'" The point, made implicitly (Dillard does not belabor it), is that you don't begin with a grand conception, either of the great American novel or a masterpiece that will hang in the Louvre. You begin with a feel for the nitty-gritty material of the medium, paint in one case, sentences in the other.

But wouldn't the equivalent of paint be words rather than sentences? Actually, no, because while you can brush or even drip paint on a canvas and make something interesting happen, just piling up words, one after the other, won't do much of anything until something else has been added. That something is named quite precisely by Anthony Burgess in this sentence from his novel *Enderby Outside* (1968):

> *And the words slide into the slots ordained by syntax,*
> *and glitter as with atmospheric dust with those impurities*
> *which we call meaning.*

Before the words slide into their slots, they are just discrete items, pointing everywhere and nowhere. Once the words are nestled in the places "ordained" for them—"ordained" is a wonderful word that points to the inexorable logic of syntactic structures—they are tied by ligatures of relationships to one another. They are subjects or objects or actions or descriptives or indications of manner, and as such they combine into a statement about the world, that is, into a meaning that one can contemplate, admire, reject, or refine. Virginia Tufte, whose book *Artful Sentences* (2006) begins with this sentence of Burgess's, comments: "It is syntax that gives the words the power to relate to each other in a sequence . . . to carry meaning—of whatever kind—as well as glow individually in just the right place." Flaubert's famous search for the "mot juste" was not a search for words that glow alone, but for words so precisely placed that in combination with other words, also precisely placed, they carve out a shape in space and time.

Here is Dillard again: "When you write you lay out a line of words. The line of words is a miner's pick, a woodcarver's gouge, a surgeon's probe. You wield it and it digs a path you follow." And when you come to the end of the path, you have a sentence. Flaubert described himself in a letter as being in a semi-diseased state, "itching with sentences." He just had to get them out. He would declaim them to passersby.

I wish I had been one of them. Some people are bird watchers, others are celebrity watchers; still others are flora and fauna watchers. I belong to the tribe of sentence watchers. Some appreciate fine art; others appreciate fine wines. I appreciate fine sentences. I am always on the lookout for sentences that take your breath away, for sentences that make you say, "Isn't that something?" or "What a sentence!" Some of my fellow sentence appreciators have websites: Best Sentences Ever, Sentences We Love, Best First Sentences, Best Last Sentences. Invariably the sentences that turn up on these sites are not chosen for the substantive political or social or philosophical points they make. They are chosen because they are performances of a certain skill at the highest level. The closest analogy, I think, is to sports highlights; you know, the five greatest dunks, or the ten greatest catches, or the fifteen greatest touchdown runbacks. The response is always, "Wasn't that amazing?" or "Can you believe it?" or "I can't for the life of me see how he did that," or "What an incredible move!" or "That's not humanly possible." And always the admiration is a rueful recognition that you couldn't do it yourself even though you also have two hands and feet. It is the same with sentences that do things the language you use every day

3

would not have seemed capable of doing. We marvel at them; we read them aloud to our friends and spouses, even, occasionally, to passersby; we analyze them; we lament our inability to match them.

One nice thing about sentences that display a skill you can only envy is that they can be found anywhere, even when you're not looking for them. I was driving home listening to NPR and heard a commentator recount a story about the legendary actress Joan Crawford. It seems that she never left the house without being dressed as if she were going to a premiere or a dinner at Sardi's. An interviewer asked her why. She replied, "If you want to see the girl next door, go next door." It is hardly surprising that Joan Crawford had thought about the importance to fans of movie stars behaving like movie stars (since her time, there has been a sea change; now, courtesy of paparazzi, we see movie stars picking up their laundry in Greenwich Village or Brentwood); what may be surprising is that she could convey her insight in a sentence one could savor. It is the bang-bang swiftness of the short imperative clause—"go next door"—that does the work by taking the commonplace phrase "the girl next door" literally and reminding us that "next door" is a real place where one should not expect to find glamour (unless of course one is watching Judy Garland singing "The Boy Next Door" in *Meet Me in St. Louis*).

A good sentence can turn up in the middle of a movie where it shines for an instant and then recedes as the plot advances. At one point in *The Magnificent Seven* (1960), the bandit leader, played by Eli Wallach, explains why he isn't bothered much by the hardships suffered by the peasant-farmers whose food and supplies he plunders:

> *If God didn't want them sheared, he would not have*
> *made them sheep.*

The sentence is snapped off, almost like the flick of a whip; it has the form of proverbial wisdom (a form we shall look at later), and the air of finality and certainty it aspires to is clinched by the parallelism of clauses that also feature the patterned repetition of consonants and vowels: "didn't want" and "would not have," "sheared" and "sheep." We know that "sheep" is coming because of "sheared" and when it arrives it seems inevitable and, at least from one perspective, just. Not bad for a bandit.

Even children can produce a good sentence. My mother-in-law, Lucille Reilly Parry, was a grade-school teacher and she recalled a day when a large box was delivered to the school. No one knew where it had come from or what it was, and she gave her fourth-grade students the assignment of writing something about it. One student began her essay with this sentence:

> *I was already on the second floor when I heard about the*
> *box.*

What is noteworthy about this sentence is its ability to draw readers in and make them want more. It is a question of what we know and don't know. We know that the writer was in the middle of something ("I was already") but we don't know what; neither do we know how she learned about the box or what effect (if any) the fact of it had on what she was in the course of doing. And so we read on in the expectation of finding out. Many practiced writers would kill for a first sentence that good.

I found another of my favorite sentences while teaching the last big school-prayer case, *Lee v. Weisman* (1992). Mr. Weisman brought a cause of action against Nathan Bishop Middle School in Providence, Rhode Island (the same school I attended many decades ago), because a thoroughly secular prayer had been read at his daughter's graduation. Weisman regarded the prayer as a breach of the First Amendment's prohibition against the state's establishing of a religion. A majority of the Supreme Court justices agreed with him and reasoned that even though the prayer had no sectarian content and made no demands on the students, who were free to ignore it, its very rehearsal was an act of "psychological coercion." This was too much for Justice Scalia, who, after citing a fellow jurist's complaint that establishment clause jurisprudence was becoming so byzantine that it was in danger of becoming a form of interior decorating, got off this zinger:

> *Interior decorating is a rock-hard science compared to psychology practiced by amateurs.*

The sentence is itself a rock thrown at Scalia's fellow justices in the majority; it is a projectile that picks up speed with every word; the acceleration is an effect of the two past participles "compared" and "practiced"; their economy does not allow a pause or a taking of a breath, and the sentence hurtles toward what is both its semantic and real-life destination: the "amateurs" who are sitting next to Scalia as he spits it out.

The pleasure I take in the sentence has nothing to do with the case or with the merits of either the majority's or the dissent's arguments. It is the pleasure of appreciating a technical achievement—here the athletic analogy might be to target shooting—in this case, Scalia's ability to load, aim, and get off a shot before his victims knew what was happening. I carry that sentence around with me as others might carry a precious gem or a fine Swiss watch. I pull it out and look at it. I pull it out and invite others (who are sometimes reluctant) to look at it. I put it under a microscope and examine its innermost workings.

That sounds, I know, rather precious, as if sentences were "one-off" performances, discrete instances of what Walter Pater sought in art, experiences of brilliant intensity that promise "nothing but the highest quality to your moments as they pass and simply for those moments' sake" (quite a sentence itself, and we shall return to Pater). But, in fact, sentences promise more. They promise nothing less than lessons and practice in the organization of the world. That is what language does: organize the world into manageable, and in some sense artificial, units that can then be inhabited and manipulated. If you can write a sentence in which actors, actions, and objects are related to one another in time, space, mood, desires, fears, causes, and effects, and if your specification of those relationships is delineated with a precision that communicates itself to your intended reader, you can, by extrapolation and expansion, write anything: a paragraph, an argument, an essay, a treatise, a novel. "There is nothing in discourse," Roland Barthes once said, "that is not to be found in a sentence" (*Image Music Text*, 1977). A discourse of any size, he added, "is a long sentence . . . just as a sentence is a short discourse." Years ago, when I was in the beginning stages of mapping out a book, my department chair, Hugh Kenner, gave me this advice: "Just get the first sentence right, everything else will follow." He meant that if my first sentence were written with a full comprehension of the twists and turns in the journey it introduced (which would make it in effect the last sentence), following its lead would guide me to the right order of my arguments and examples. He was right.

A sentence is, in John Donne's words, "a little world made cunningly." (Donne is speaking of the human body, but that is just another composition.) I want to bring you into the little worlds made cunningly by as many writers as I can cram into a short book. My motives are at once aesthetic and practical. I hope that you will come to share the delight and awe I feel when reading and contemplating these sentences, and I hope that by the time you finish you will be able to write some fine, if not great, sentences yourself. So I promise to give you both sentence pleasure and sentence craft, the ability to appreciate a good sentence and the ability to fashion one. These skills are sometimes thought of as having only an oblique relationship to one another, but they are, I believe, acquired in tandem. If you learn what it is that goes into the making of a memorable sentence—what skills of coordination, subordination, allusion, compression, parallelism, alliteration (all terms to be explained later) are in play—you will also be learning how to take the appreciative measure of such sentences. And conversely, if you can add to your admiration of a sentence an analytical awareness of what caused you to admire it, you will be that much farther down the road of being able to produce one (somewhat) like it.

And there is a third benefit: practice in the analyzing and imitating of sentences is also practice in the reading of sentences. In general, of course, reading is easier than writing. Almost anyone can read with pleasure the sentence in which John Updike tells us what it was like to see Ted Williams—the Kid, the Splendid Splinter—hit a home run in his last at bat in Fenway Park on September 28, 1960:

*It was in the books while it was still in the sky.*

But it takes a little bit more to talk precisely about what makes the sentence so effective. The fulcrum of the sentence is "while"; on either side of it are two apparently very different kinds of observations. "It was in the books" is metaphorical. Updike imagines, correctly, that this moment will be memorialized in stories and at the Baseball Hall of Fame in Cooperstown, New York, and he confers that mythical status on the moment before it is completed, before the ball actually goes out of the park. Indeed, in his sentence the ball never does get out of the park. It is "still in the sky," a phrase that has multiple meanings; the ball is still in the sky in the sense that it has not yet landed; it is still in the sky in the sense that its motion is arrested; and it is still in the sky in the sense that it is, and will remain forever, in the sky of the books, in the record of the game's highest, most soaring achievements. On the surface "in the book" and "in the sky" are in distinct registers, one referring to the monumentality the home run will acquire in history, the other describing the ball's actual physical arc; but the registers are finally, and indeed immediately (this sentences goes fast), the same: the physical act and its transformation into myth occur simultaneously; or rather, that is what Updike makes us feel as we glide through this deceptively simple sentence composed entirely of monosyllables.

How hard is it to write a sentence like Updike's? Well, let's try. What you need is a hinge word that ostensibly separates distinct temporal states, but actually brings them together to the point where there is no temporal distance between them. Here is my (relatively feeble) attempt: "It was in my stomach before it was off the shelf." Now, I'm not going to make any great claims for my sentence, but I will say that it is a game attempt to approach Updike's art by imitating it, by arranging clauses in somewhat the same way he does in order to achieve a somewhat similar, if decidedly minor, effect. And once you get the hang of it—of zeroing in on a form that can then be filled with any number of contents—you can do it forever. "She was enrolled at Harvard before she was conceived." "He had won the match before the first serve." "They were celebrating while the other team was still at bat."

Part of my thesis, as I have already suggested, is that the exercise of analyzing Updike's sentence and then trying to match it will have a payoff when you go back and read it. Understanding how it is that he produced a complex effect will make that effect more available to you as a reader. You might have a sense of how good it is before you take it apart, but taking it apart will give you an enhanced understanding of just what kind of goodness it performs. My wife is a serious painter. When she and I go to a gallery we might both be impressed by the same painting, but she will be able to tell me, in analytical detail, what makes it impressive, how the painter did it. So it is with writing: the practice of analyzing and imitating sentences is also the practice of learning how to read them with an informed appreciation. Here's the formula:

> *Sentence craft equals sentence comprehension equals sentence appreciation.*

My last sentence uses the word "sentence" three times, and in this sentence I have now done the same. Indeed a large number of the sentences I have written so far have the word "sentence" in them; and yet I have not answered or even asked the basic question: What is a sentence, anyway? It is to that question that we now turn.

# CHAPTER 2

# WHY YOU WON'T
# FIND THE ANSWER
# IN STRUNK AND WHITE

STRUNK AND WHITE'S *The Elements of Style* (1959, 2000) long ago attained the status of a classic. Millions of copies sold, countless accolades, including this one from the *Boston Globe*: "No book in shorter space, with fewer words, will help any writer more than this persistent little volume"; and this one from the *St. Paul Dispatch*: "This excellent book, which should go off to college with every freshman, is recognized as the best book of its kind we have." No doubt this praise is deserved if the person using the book already knows how to write; already knows, that is, what a sentence is. For then advice like "Do not join independent clauses with a comma" and "The number of the subject determines the number of the verb" will be genuinely helpful. But if you're not quite sure what a sentence is (and isn't) and you understand the words "number," "subject," and "verb" but couldn't for the life of you explain how they go together or what an independent clause is, Strunk and White's instructions will make no sense.

In short, Strunk and White's advice assumes a level of knowledge and understanding only some of their readers will have attained; the vocabulary they confidently offer is itself in need of an analysis and explanation they do not provide. And this is true too of the other guides that promise improvement in a short time, like the guide that tells you on the first page that "a sentence is the building block of verbal and written communication" (true; but how is the building done and when does it add up to communication?), and then announces magisterially, but unhelpfully, that sentences "are built with eight different kinds of words called the parts of speech" (Joanne Kimes and Gary Robert Muschla, *Grammar Sucks: What to Do to Make Your Writing Much More Better*, 2007). The eight parts duly follow ("noun, pronoun, verb, adjective, adverb, preposition, conjunction, and interjection"), and all at once the terms the reader doesn't understand have multiplied by eight. With each part of speech comes a list of errors you can, and probably will, make while trying to deploy it; obscurity of reference (what are these things, anyway?) is joined by fear, and the goal of being comfortable with the task of writing recedes into the distance. The very thought of putting pen to paper, an anachronism I find hard to let go of, is enough to bring on an anxiety attack.

I have just reproduced one of the standard arguments against learning to write by studying forms. For decades researchers have been telling us that "the teaching of formal grammar has a negligible or . . . even a harmful effect on the teaching of writing" (Richard Braddock, Richard Lloyd-Jones, Lowell Schoer, *Research in Written Composition*, 1963). I agree if by "the teaching of formal grammar" is meant memorizing the parts of speech or rehearsing the distinction between dependent and independent clauses or listing the uses of the subjunctive. That kind of rote knowledge is merely taxonomic. It explains nothing; students who acquire it have learned nothing about how to write, and it is no surprise when research demonstrates its nonutility.

The conclusion to be drawn, however, is not that focusing on forms is irrelevant to the act of composing, but that the focus one finds in the grammar books is on the wrong forms, on forms detached from the underlying (or overarching) form that must be in place before any technical terms can be meaningful or alive. That underlying form is the sentence itself, and even though it might seem to go without saying, let me say it again: If it is your goal is to write well-constructed sentences, it makes sense to begin by asking the basic and, one would have thought, obvious question "What *is* a sentence, anyway?" The writing guides certainly offer answers to that question; they say, variously, "a sentence is a complete thought" or "a sentence contains a subject and a predicate" or "sentences consist of one or more clauses that bear certain relationships to one another" (Anita K. Barry, *English Grammar: Language as Human Behavior*, 2002). But, far from being transparent and incisive, these declarations come wrapped in a fog; they seem to skate on their own surface and simply don't go deep enough.

And what can I offer that will go deeper? Well, my bottom line can be summarized in two statements: (1) a sentence is an organization of items in the world; and (2) a sentence is a structure of logical relationships. The first statement is insufficiently helpful because it is overbroad: lists, dictionaries, encyclopedias, library card catalogues, bedroom bureaus, and file cabinets also organize items in the world. What is distinctive about the organization a sentence performs? The answer is given in statement (2); it is a *logical* organization, an assertion that is also overbroad, but one that can be refined and narrowed with the help of an exercise. Look around the room you are now in and pick out four or five items. Then add a verb or a modal auxiliary (would, should, could, must, may, might, shall, can, will). Finally, make a sentence out of what you have. (You will of course have to add words.) My list is "pen," "chair," "garbage can," "printer," and "shall," and my first try at a sentence is "Before using the printer I shall remove the pen from the chair and throw it in the garbage can." Other sentences might be, "I shall move the garbage can so that I can pull the chair up to the printer and have access to my pen," or "I shall set the printer on the chair and get my pen out of the garbage can."

Notice first that the number of sentences that could be made out of these components is theoretically infinite. Or, to put it another way, any number of contents (little stories or narratives) can be fashioned out of these meager materials. We shall return to the question of content—what exactly it is and what its relationship to form is—but first I want to pose an apparently simple question: What is it that we do when we make a sentence out of a random collection of words? What is it that we add to those words that causes them to form something we recognize as a sentence? The answer can be given in a single word, and that word is "relationships." In my third sentence— "I shall set the printer on the chair and get my pen out of the garbage can"—each of the words in the original list now exists in a logical relation to the others. "Shall" is now joined to a verb, "set," to form an action; "printer" is now the object of that action, which is performed by "I"; "chair" is now part of a prepositional phrase (a phrase temporally and spatially relating objects to one another)—"upon the chair"—which names the place where the action of setting occurs. "And" introduces a sequence that is, structurally, a mirror image of what precedes it. "Pen" is the object of "shall get" and "out of the garbage can" names the place where and the manner in which the pen has been gotten. No word floats without an anchoring connection within an overall structure.

A poem by Kenneth Koch captures the exercise, its requirements, and its point:

> One day the Nouns were clustered in the street.
> An Adjective walked by, with her dark beauty
> The Nouns were struck, moved, changed.
> The next day a Verb drove up, and created the Sentence.
>
> ("Permanently," 1960)

Alone a word is just a word, a part of speech clustered in a category; it looks over at other words it would like to have a relationship with (it's almost a dating situation) but has no way of connecting with them. And then a verb shows up, providing a way of linking up noun to adjective, and suddenly you have a sentence, a proposition, a little world. "Beautiful Joan sighed." "John was angry." "I am proud." "Crucial decisions await." And on and on forever.

It is important to understand that the relationships that form the sinews and relays of sentences are limited. There is the person or thing performing an action, there is the action being performed, and there is the recipient or object of the action. That's the basic logical structure of many sentences: X does Y to Z. (Sentences can also come without objects, as in "Joe walks.") "Simon bought the car." "The government raised taxes." "The corporation gives bonuses." "Heat parches lawns." The instances are infinite, although the form remains the same (this is a key point, and I shall return to it): doer, doing, done to.

It's not the number of words that renders these and millions of other sentences structurally interchangeable, but the relationships between the words. That is why "Simon drinks slowly" doesn't fit the pattern: "slowly" isn't the object of the action "drink"; rather it gives information about the act of drinking; it says how the drinking is done; it is done slowly. That is what words and phrases that don't point to a sentence's main components do; they give information about them. In the sentence "Before using the printer I shall remove the chair and throw it into the garbage can," "Before using the printer" gives information about when the action of removing occurred, and "into the garbage" gives information about where the action of throwing ends up. In the sentence "Arriving at the house, I opened the car windows," "Arriving at the house" gives information about the actor "I." Who am I? I'm the one arriving at the house. In the sentence "Determined to win, he laid down a hard body block," "Determined to win" gives information about the person who lays down the block. "Hard" gives information about the body block. What kind of body block is it? A hard body block.

Now of course you can give these words, phrases, and clauses technical names. You can call them "prepositional phrases," as I did in the previous paragraph; you can call them past or present participles; you can call them adverbs; you can call them nouns; you can call them adjectives. And you can subdivide these terms and produce ever finer distinctions. But to what end? You can know what the eight parts of speech are, and even be able to apply the labels correctly, and still not understand anything about the way a sentence works. Technical knowledge, divorced from what it is supposed to be knowledge of, yields only the illusion of understanding. It's like being able to reel off the locations on a baseball field—first base, second base, third base, home plate, left field, right field, center field, pitcher's mound—without having the slightest clue as to how they function in a game. You can talk the talk, but you can't walk the walk.

Not only is that kind of abstract knowledge unhelpful, it is often misleading, for it deceives those who possess it into thinking they know more than they do. Nine times out of ten when I ask someone to pick out the verb (the designator of the action) in the sentence "Helping old ladies cross the street prevents accidents," the first answer I will hear is "Helping" and the second I will hear is "cross." And were I to ask what is the sentence's subject (an unhappy grammatical term because it suggests theme or content), the answer most likely would be "old ladies." People make these mistakes because they think that whenever something they recognize as a noun turns up, it must be the subject of the sentence, or that whenever they recognize a verbal form, it must be the sentence's main verb. They confuse a taxonomy of the parts of speech with an analysis of a sentence's logical structure. The two are entirely distinct. You can't tell anything about the function a word plays in a sentence by identifying it as a noun or a verb. "Old ladies" is certainly a noun (or more precisely a noun phrase), and "Helping" and "cross" are certainly verbal forms, but the subject of the sentence is whatever performs its action, and in this case it is the compound phrase "Helping old ladies cross the street"; the main verb of the sentence is whatever action is being performed, and in this case it is the action "prevents."

A little while back I observed that many people are put off writing because they fear committing one or more of the innumerable errors that seem to lie in wait for them at every step of composition. But if one understands that a sentence is a structure of logical relationships and that the number of relationships involved is finite, one understands too that there is only one error to worry about, the error of being illogical, and only one rule to follow: make sure that every component of your sentences is related to the other components in a way that is clear and unambiguous (unless ambiguity is what you are aiming at). And how do you do that? Not by learning rules, but by coming to know the limited number of relationships your words, phrases, and clauses can enter into, and becoming alert to those times when the relationships are not established or are unclear: when a phrase just dangles in space, when a connective has nothing to connect to, when a prepositional phrase is in search of a verb to complement, when a pronoun cannot be paired with a noun.

These are all errors catalogued in traditional grammar texts, but the catalogue really has only one entry marked "doesn't link to anything" or "has too many possible links" or "is off in a corner by itself," or "stands outside the sentence's logic" or "undoes the sentence's logic." What happens when a sentence goes out of control or was never under control in the first place is that it ceases being a sentence and returns to the state when its parts made up nothing more cohesive than a random list. The exercise I introduced a few paragraphs ago—grab five items out of the air and make them into a sentence—can be reversed and is reversed whenever the components of the sentence you are trying to write seem to be independent of one another. (Hey, I'm an adjective, but I don't have anything to modify; can anyone help me?) The achievement of organization has been undone, and what is left is (once again) just a collection of unrelated words, like the words standing isolated on a street corner at the beginning of Kenneth Koch's poem.

How can you tell when that is happening? Just ask. Scrutinize every part of your sentence and ask, "What does it go with?" or "What does it support?" or "What information does it give about some other part?" or "What is it referring to?"—all variations of the master question, "How does it fit into the sentence's logical structure?" If at any point you can't come up with an answer, you know you're in trouble and you know what the trouble is or at least where it is located, and you can begin to go about addressing it.

Of course this advice can be followed only if you are sensitive to the presence of a problem, if you sense that something has gone wrong. How is that sensitivity acquired? By performing exercises that hone it, like the exercise of making a sentence out of a random list of words. Everyone can do it. The hard part—and the part that will firm up your sense of the logical structure of sentences—is explaining what it is that you have done. The general answer is that you have inserted the words into a structure of relationships. But the general answer is too general to be useful. If the exercise is to be helpful beyond the moment of its performance, you have to step back reflectively and specify what role each word or phrase you have added to the list plays in the formation of a logical structure. You have to be able to say (if only to yourself) things like, "When I added this verb, I made this previously random and stand-alone word into the object of an action," or "When I added this prepositional phrase I located the action in a particular space." Turning this corner will be difficult; it's a lot easier to form sentences than to produce an analysis of your ability to do so. But after a little while and a lot of practice, you will have internalized a grammatical "sixth sense" that enables you first to sense that something has gone wrong and then to zero in on it, and finally to correct it.

As with any skill, this one develops slowly. You start small, with three-word sentences, and after you've advanced to the point where you can rattle off their structure on demand, you go on to the next step and another exercise. Take a little sentence ("Bob collects coins" or "John hit the ball"), whose ensemble of relationships you are now able to explain in your sleep, and expand it, first into a sentence of fifteen words and then into a sentence of thirty words, and finally, into a sentence of one hundred words—all the while never losing contact with the "doer-doing-done to" structure you began with. And then—here comes the hard part again—tag every added component with an account of how it functions to extend and maintain the set of relationships that holds the sentence, however mammoth or unwieldy it becomes, together.

Here, for example, is the sentence "John hit the ball" pumped up into something unreadable but perfectly formed:

> In the middle of the sixth inning of a crucial game in the pennant race, John, the league leader batting third, weakly but precisely hit on the nose the ball pitched with great velocity by the sure-to-be Hall of Fame hurler who had won his last five starts in an overwhelming fashion while going the whole nine innings and who therefore presented an intimidating image to anyone facing him, especially as the shadows lengthened over the mound, obscuring the mechanics of his delivery and rendering it difficult even to see the spheroid as it curved its sinuous way toward the plate, behind which were the umpire, ready to say "ball" or "strike," and the catcher, prepared for whatever was about to happen.

Constructing this monster is easy, and I have found that

freshman students have no trouble doing something similar with the three-word sentences of their choice. Giving an analytical account of how the construction was accomplished takes more work, and would require, for example, coming to see (and explaining) that everything following the word "ball" is a modification of it. What ball is it? It is the ball "pitched with great velocity by the sure-to-be Hall of Fame hurler who." Everything from "who" to "anyone facing him" modifies or describes or characterizes the hurler (who, we must remember, has been brought in to further specify what ball it is that has been hit). Everything from "especially" to the end of the sentence modifies or fleshes out the intimidating image the hurler presents. And everything remains tethered to the word "ball," the object of "hit," the action performed by John, whose biography precedes his appearance in the sentence. Within the overall structure there are all the smaller units, like "as the shadows lengthened over the mound," and they too have their own internal structure that must also be explicated. (A full analysis of this sentence would fill many pages.)

The more times you perform this exercise, always with different three-word sentences as the base, the easier it becomes, and the easier it becomes, the more practiced you will be in spotting the structure of relationships that gives sense and coherence even to verbal behemoths like this one.

# CHAPTER 3

# IT'S NOT THE THOUGHT
# THAT COUNTS

NOTICE THAT IT doesn't matter which three-word sentence you use as a base. It doesn't matter what the sentences you practice with say; it doesn't matter what their content is. In fact, the less interesting the sentences are in their own right the more useful they are as vehicles of instruction, because, as you work with them, you will not be tempted to focus on their content and you will be able to pay attention to the structural relationships that make content—any content—possible. The conventional wisdom is that content comes first—"you have to write about *something*" is the usual commonplace—but if what you want to do is learn how to compose sentences, content must take a backseat to a mastery of the forms without which you can't say anything in the first place.

To be sure, your eventual goal is to be able to write forcefully about issues that matter to you, but if you begin with those issues uppermost in your mind, you will never get to the point where you can do verbal justice to them. It may sound paradoxical, but verbal fluency is the product of hours spent writing about nothing, just as musical fluency is the product of hours spent repeating scales. For the purposes of becoming a facile (in the positive sense) writer of sentences, the sentences you practice with should have as little meaning as possible. Indeed, nonsense sentences—sentences that display a logical arrangement of components, but are without a readily discernible message—may be the best materials. The linguist Noam Chomsky famously offered the sequence "colorless green ideas sleep furiously" as an example of a verbal unit that is perfectly grammatical but semantically nonsensical. It is grammatical because the doer (ideas), and the doing (sleep), along with the manner of the doing (furiously), are in the appropriate structural slots. It is nonsensical (or so it is said; were it a line in a Wallace Stevens poem, sense would be attributed to it in a heartbeat) because ideas do not sleep, and sleep is a quiescent activity rather than an activity that can be performed furiously. It is a well-formed structure without meaning.

Chomsky contrasts "colorless green ideas sleep furiously" with "furiously sleep ideas green colorless," which, because it exhibits no logical relationships whatsoever, is a list of the kind I presented in my first example. You can work with "colorless green ideas sleep furiously" by treating it as a formal structure with "slots" that can be filled with alternative words (e.g., "mystical white filaments exfoliate silently"), and you can learn something about what makes a sentence a sentence by maintaining that structure in the face of serial nonsense. You can't do anything with "furiously sleep ideas green colorless," not because it is without meaning, but because it is without form. It is true that you can't get from form to content, but it is also true that without form, content cannot emerge. When it comes to formulating a proposition, form comes first; forms are generative not of specific meanings, but of the very possibility of meaning. Despite the familiar proverb, it's not the thought that counts. Form, form, form, and only form is the road to what the classical theorists called "invention," the art of coming up with something to say. It follows that familiarizing yourself with form independent of any content you might want to elaborate later is the way to learn how to write a sentence.

Here's another exercise that will illustrate the point. Begin with the first stanza of Lewis Carroll's "Jabberwocky":

> 'Twas brillig, and the slithy toves
> Did gyre and gimble in the wabe;
> All mimsy were the borogoves,
> And the mome raths outgrabe.

Now replace the nonsense words with good English words in a way that leads to a meaningful sequence. The exercise is useful because there is no content guiding your performance of it. All you have are forms, but they are enough. If you are a speaker of English you know—although it is the kind of knowledge you may never have articulated—that there are only certain classes of words that can follow " 'Twas." "Exciting," "evening," "unfinished," "urban," "Texas," or "hilarious" would be okay, but "did"—" 'Twas did"—would not (unless you were e.e. cummings). You know, to be a bit more technical, that a "linking verb" such as "was" introduces a state or a condition or a location but does not introduce a verbal auxiliary such as "did." That knowledge, which, again, is formal, constrains what can replace "brillig," but within that constraint the possibilities are vast. Formal knowledge also tells you that the phrase "the slithy toves" will be composed of a noun and an adjective ("the whispering breezes," "the agitated monkeys," "the unhappy suburbanites," "the beautiful lilies") and not of two nouns ("the whispers breezes") or two adjectives ("the agitated beautiful," as opposed to "the agitated beauty," which is fine). In exactly the same way, you know that "did" accompanies and specifies the tense or time frame of verbs, so that "gyre and gimble" can be replaced by "sway and bounce" or "breath and shine" or a thousand other combinations, but not by "high and low" or "bright and cheery."

Making these substitutions is the easy part. Explaining how you knew how to do it is harder, because it requires bringing to the surface of your analytical consciousness inferences you have made without thinking about them. But it is that extra step that will put you into meaningful contact with the world of forms and help you begin the journey that will end with your being a fully enfranchised and informed citizen of that world.

Let me say again that by "forms" I do not mean parts of speech or any other bit of abstract machinery. I mean structures of logic and rhetoric within which and by means of which meanings—lots of them—can be generated. The logical structures are the ones we have already met: the structure of relationships between actor, actions, and the objects acted upon. The rhetorical structures are structures of argument (that is what rhetoric is, the art of argument); they too are formal—abstract, contentless—but rather than being the forms that make random words into propositions (sentences), they are forms that link propositions together in more complex units. Relationships are also central to their operation, but they are relationships among statements, not the relationships that must be in place if there are to be statements at all.

Gerald Graff and Cathy Birkenstein call these forms of argument "templates." The title of their book, *They Say/I Say* (2006), identifies one of them. Speakers and writers who can deploy this template know how to summarize conventional wisdom on a topic on the way to disagreeing with it. "They say that money talks, but I say money corrupts." You might think that disagreeing is a "natural" act, requiring no formal skills. But disagreeing is a learned activity; it is more than just saying no; it involves giving reasons for your rejection of what others have said. As Graff and Birkenstein put it, "they say/I say" enables writers not only to make claims, but also to "map those claims relative to the claims of others." Organizing a discourse around views you oppose is an achievement of artifice, and it is made possible by a form you have to acquire through practice.

Although the forms of argument are more numerous than the forms of sentence structure, their number is limited; they can be catalogued (Graff and Birkenstein do it), they can be added to your argumentative repertoire, and you can use them not simply to arrange thoughts but also to create thoughts. Creativity is often contrasted with forms to the latter's detriment, but the truth is that forms are the engines of creativity. "Our templates," say Graff and Birkenstein, "have a generative quality, prompting students to make moves in their writing they might not otherwise make or even know they should make" or (I would add) even know they could make. "When we ask students to write sentences using the form 'at this point you probably object that'—they invariably come up with objections—content—that had never occurred to them and they would never have written on their own."

The same thing will happen if you give yourself the assignment of writing a sentence in which three or even four time zones—past perfect, past, present, future—are structured into an account of related actions. You can start with any simple proposition, say, "We ate the pizza"; and then imagine a prior event, "After we had finished the job"; and then imagine an event in the present, "and now we're getting ready to go home"; and finally move on to the future, "where we will finish the day eating ice cream." Or you can start with a contrary-to-fact construction like "Had I been there," and give yourself the task of completing the sentence using at least two additional tenses. "Had I been there, I would have prevented them from doing it and now I will have to clean up their mess." You can come to this exercise from any direction—from a future tense assertion from which you have to move backward in time: "I will do this, although long before you proposed it, I had already made up my mind"; from a present assertion: "I reject the idea" to prior and future events: "because you didn't consult with me, I reject the idea and will consider other options." There is no end to the variations you can run on this exercise, and in any of the variations, the point will not be the content but the formal requirement—"write a sentence with the following features"—that produces it.

You can get even more basic. Give yourself the assignment of completing a sentence that begins "Had I." Examples might be "Had I known you were coming I would have baked a cake," "Had I read the book I would be able to answer the question," and "Had I not been there, I wouldn't be so afraid." Now ask yourself how many contents are there that could fill this form? The answer is an infinite number. How many forms are there? Only one. Then the hard question: What is the form? What exactly is a "Had I" sentence? What do you know about a sentence the moment you hear or read the words "Had I"? It will take some time to come up with the answer, but in the end you'll get it, and it will be something like this: In a "Had I" sentence, an action taken or not taken in the past will be related causally to an action you did or did not take at a later point or in the present. This very abstract account is an account of form; as a form, it is empty, but precisely because it is empty—not hostage to any particular content—it serves as a mold into which innumerable contents can be poured. There is no limit to the forms you can practice in this way: "Even though," "Were I to,"

"Notwithstanding that," "Depending on whether," "In the event that." Each of these forms exists to make available a certain content, and apart from them, that content could not be briskly produced. An "Even though" sentence—"Even though I was exhausted, I watched another episode of *Law & Order*"—makes a complicated statement: it specifies two actions that follow one another but, in the usual course of things, shouldn't (if I'm exhausted I should turn off the TV), and it signals awareness of the oddness of the sequence even before we know exactly what its specifics are. Without the "Even though" at the beginning of the sentence, you'd have two propositions in tension; with it, the tension is acknowledged before the propositions emerge. Just as you know what words can fill the slots in Carroll's "Jabberwocky" simply by attending to the poem's skeletal form, so do you know what kind of relationship between propositions will follow when the first two words of a sentence are "Even though."

A famous sonnet by William Wordsworth begins, "Nuns fret not at their convent's narrow room; / And hermits are contented with their cells; / and students with their pensive citadels." Wordsworth's point is that what nuns, hermits, and students do is facilitated rather than hindered by the confines of the formal structures they inhabit; because those structures constrain freedom (they remove, says Wordsworth, "the weight of too much liberty"), they enable movements in a defined space. If the moves you can perform are prescribed and limited—if, for example, every line in your poem must have ten syllables and rhyme according to a predetermined pattern—each move can carry a precise significance. If, on

the other hand, there are an infinite number of moves to perform, the significance of any one of them may be difficult to
discern. (This is one of the insights of information theory.)
That is why Wordsworth reports himself happy "to be bound
/ Within the Sonnet's scanty plot of ground." It is a scanty
plot because it is bounded, and because it is bounded, it can
be the generator of boundless meanings.

This, then, is my theology: *You shall tie yourself to forms and
the forms shall set you* free. I call this the Karate Kid method
of learning how to write. In the 1984 cult movie (recently
remade), the title figure is being trained to perform in a
match, but rather than being instructed in a match's rhythms
and demands, he is asked by his teacher to practice polishing
cars ("wax on, wax off") and painting fences. Although the
kid thinks he isn't learning anything, he is learning everything; he is learning the formal motions that, when actual
combat occurs, will come to him naturally. Like the verbal
forms that enable thought and meaning, these physical forms
enable action in a sequence, even though they are essentially
static and abstract. Know what makes a sentence more than
a random list, practice constructing sentences and explaining what you have done, and you will know how to make
sentences forever and you will know too when what you are
writing doesn't make the grade because it has degenerated
into a mere pile of discrete items.

CHAPTER 4

# WHAT IS A GOOD SENTENCE?

BUT EVEN IF you follow my advice and become adept at producing well-formed sentences and at diagnosing ill-formed ones, you are only halfway home. You may be able to write a sentence; you still have to learn how to write a *good* sentence, and before you can do that, you have to know what a good sentence is. And this is where content, banished from the discussion so far, comes roaring back in. Content, the communication in a thrilling and effective way of ideas and passions, is finally what sentences are for. But just as you can't produce a sophisticated meal without a thorough knowledge of ingredients, seasonings, sauces, temperatures, utensils, pots, pans, and much more, so you can't produce powerful content in the shape of sentences that take your readers by storm without having a command of the devices—formal devices—that are at once content's vehicles and generators. Those devices make the enterprise go, but they are not, except for linguists and grammarians and sentence nuts like me, ends in themselves. The end, the goal, the aspiration is to say something, and the something you want to say will be the measure of whether you have written a sentence that is not only coherent but good.

"Good," however, is a measure that cannot be reduced to a set of features or a taxonomy. You can't produce a good sentence—a sentence not only well formed but memorable— by consulting a recipe. Indeed, even a bad sentence—a sentence that creaks or is clumsy or is overblown or is impossibly loose—can be a good sentence. There's an NPR program called *The Annoying Music Show,* and when the remastered set of Beatles albums came out in 2009, an episode was built around it. The cuts played included Tiny Tim singing "Hey Jude" and Telly (Kojak) Savalas singing "Something in the Way She Walks." These performances were truly bad and they were truly good. They were bad because in both instances the voice, the pace, and the intonation were all wrong for the song; hearing the Beatles' version in the background of these dismal renditions was painful. But the performances were good for the same reason. The *point* of playing the cuts— not the point of recording them originally—was to provoke just such a counterpoint in the listener's mind. That's what makes the whole thing funny; and if it's funny, it's good, at least in the context of *The Annoying Music Show.*

The important word in the previous sentence is "context"

and it should be paired with another, "purpose." People write or speak sentences in order to produce an effect, and the success of a sentence is measured by the degree to which the desired effect has been achieved. That is why the prescriptive advice you often get in books like Strunk and White's *The Elements of Style*—write short sentences, be direct, don't get lost in a maze of piled-up clauses, avoid the passive voice, place yourself in the background, employ figures of speech sparingly—is useful only in relation to some purposes, and unfortunate in relation to others. The first thing to ask when writing a sentence is "What am I trying to do?"

The answers are innumerable (that is why examples, not rules, are what learning to write requires), but one of them won't be "to tell it like it is." It is often said that the job of language is to report or reflect or mirror reality, but the power of language is greater and more dangerous than that; it shapes reality, not of course in a literal sense—the world is one thing, words another—but in the sense that the order imposed on a piece of the world by a sentence is only one among innumerable possible orders. Think about what you do when you revise a sentence: You add something, you delete something, you substitute one tense for another, you rearrange clauses and phrases; and with each change, the "reality" offered to your readers changes. An attempt to delineate in words even the smallest moment—a greeting in the street, the drinking of a cup of coffee, the opening of a window—necessarily leaves out more than it includes, whether you write a sentence of twenty words or two thousand. There is always another detail or an alternative perspective or a different emphasis that might have been brought in and, by being brought in, altered the snapshot of reality you are presenting. This does not mean that your sentences are always incomplete and that you should strive to cram them full of everything in the universe on the model of what Molly Bloom does in the monologue from Joyce's *Ulysses*. Sentence writers are not copyists; they are selectors. It is impossible not to select when you are making an assertion. The goal is not to be comprehensive, to say everything that could possibly be said to the extent that no one could say anything else; if that were the goal, no sentence could ever be finished. The goal is to communicate forcefully whatever perspective or emphasis or hierarchy of concerns attaches to your present purposes.

In his great book *How to Do Things with Words* (1962), J. L. Austin considers the apparently simple sentence "France is hexagonal." He asks if this is true or false, a question that makes perfect sense if the job of a sentence is to be faithful to the world. His answer is that it depends. If you are a general contemplating a coming battle, saying that France is hexagonal might help you assess various military options of defense and attack; it would be a good sentence. But if you are a geographer charged with the task of mapping France's contours, saying that France is hexagonal might cost you your union card; a greater degree of detail and fineness of scale is required of mapmakers. "France is hexagonal," Austin explains, is true "for certain intents and purposes" and false or inadequate or even nonsensical for others. It is, he says, a matter of the "dimension of assessment"—that is, a matter of what is the "right or proper thing to say as opposed to a wrong thing in these circumstances, to this audience, for these purposes and with these intentions."

How many dimensions of assessment—of purposive contexts within which assertion occurs—are there? The inventory would be endless. There is the military dimension of assessment and the mapmaker's dimension of assessment and the political dimension of assessment and the economic dimension of assessment and the domestic dimension of assessment and on and on. It is within these dimensions of assessment that any assertion or sentence is uttered, and it is within these dimensions of assessment that the objects to which sentences "refer" come into view. I put "refer" in quotation marks because the word implies that the object comes into view apart from whatever is said about it. That implication is wrong. You can say what France is like from a culinary perspective or an energy perspective or an agricultural perspective, or myriad other perspectives, but you can't say what France is like from no perspective or dimension of assessment whatsoever. The question "What is France really like?" cannot be answered if by "really" is meant independently of any vocabulary that might be employed to describe or characterize it. What we know of the world comes to us through words, or, to look at it from the other direction, when we write a sentence, we create a world, which is not *the* world, but the world as is appears within a dimension of assessment. When I said earlier that a sentence is an organization of items in the world, I intended the word "organization" strongly: it is an organization that shapes the items it gathers in by relating them to each other in some ways, but not in all ways. The skill it takes to produce a sentence—the skill of linking events, actions, and objects in a strict logic—is also the skill of creating a world.

Philosopher Nelson Goodman calls this process of creative representation "ways of worldmaking." We commonly call those ways "styles." "Style" is a word that is often understood as one member of an opposed pair: "style versus content," or "style versus meaning," or "style versus substance." In these binary formulations the non-style pole is usually the favored one—content over style, meaning over style, substance over style. The suggestion is that style is not only secondary and parasitic; it is meretricious, and it would be better if we did without it. When Aristotle introduces the subject of style in Book III of his *Rhetoric*, he does so apologetically. I would like, he says, to advise you to present your case "with no help beyond the bare facts," but given the tendency of men and women to be influenced by emotional appeals and the tricks of eloquence, it is necessary to give instruction in the arts of rhetoric. No one, Aristotle declares plaintively, "uses fine language when teaching geometry," because geometry is a system of pure forms.

Aristotle initiates a tradition in which the desire is to make language so transparent a medium that it disappears and interposes no obstacle or screen between the reader and the things it points to. The Roman Cato made the point with characteristic brevity: "Seize the thing, the words will follow" (*rem tene, verba sequentur*), where "follow" should be taken literally: words come after, not before. In the seventeenth century, Bishop Thomas Sprat of the Royal Society proposed that "eloquence . . . be banished out of all civil societies" because the ornaments of speech "are in open defiance against reason" (*History of the Royal Society*, 1667) and are allied instead with the passions. In the eighteenth century, Jonathan Swift took this idea to its logical and absurd conclusion when his Gulliver reports on the "scheme" undertaken by the Academy of Lagado "for entirely abolishing all words whatsoever" (*Gulliver's Travels*, 1726, 1735). Since words only stand in for things and have the unhappy tendency of substituting themselves for the things they should represent, "it would be more convenient," say the academicians, "for all men to carry about them such things as were necessary to express the particular business they are to discourse on." Gulliver observes (and behind him we can hear the mocking voice of Swift) that a major liability attends this project: the man who engages in it "must be obliged . . . to carry a greater bundle of things upon his back." Indeed, Gulliver recalls, "I have often beheld two of those sages almost sinking under the weight of their packs . . . who when they met in the streets, would lay down their loads, open their sacks, and hold conversation for an hour together." This would be a very limited conversation, extending only to the display of discrete items. If the "sages" wanted to relate these items in some way—subordinate one to another or arrange them in a sequence of cause and effect or rank them in a scale of usefulness or value—the machinery of predication complete with tenses, moods, modifiers, adversative conjunctions, adverbs, and much more would have to be employed. Once that machinery was set in motion, the "pure" world of things, so dear to the heart of the Catos and Sprats of the world, would have receded and become components in language's structure, the structure that would have given those things the meanings they do not possess in and of themselves.

What Swift is telling us with his characteristic wit is that the dream of doing without words will never be realized as long as we desire to produce complex statements rather than mere lists. Language is not a handmaiden to perception; it *is* perception; it gives shape to what would otherwise be inert and dead. The shaping power of language cannot be avoided. We cannot choose to distance ourselves from it. We can only choose to employ it in one way rather than another. We can only choose our style, not choose to abandon style, and it behooves us to know what the various styles in our repertoire are for and what they can do.

This form of knowledge is very old and it has been codified many times. The classic codification is Cicero's three-part taxonomy: the grand or ornamental style, the middle style, and the low or plain style. The grand style is ceremonial or exhortative; the middle style is conversational and amiable; the plain style is unadorned and suitable for explaining and teaching. The styles are sometimes correlated with subject matter; the grand style for the most important things, the middle for matters of everyday concerns, the low style for inconsequential matters. And still another correlation is with effect, depending on whether you want to move your audience, please your audience, or instruct your audience. Because these distinctions were taught in the schools and known to all literate readers, the very choice of a style says something even before anything substantive is said. Cicero's audience knows what it's in for when he begins his *First Oration Against Catiline*

(63 B.C.) with these famous words: "How long, O Catiline, will you abuse our patience, how long will that madness of yours mock us?" We don't give formal orations anymore, but we do rise to speak at meetings, and we do give welcoming remarks on a variety of occasions, and we do (some of us do) address juries in opening and closing statements, and we do write letters of application and nomination. In these and many other contexts, the first step in producing good sentences is to decide what style you will use to communicate your message, a decision that sends a message of its own.

Cicero's classifications are canonical—they have had a long life—but they are not exhaustive and they do not correspond to eternal types. They codify conventional practices—time-honored correlations of formal features and purposive contexts—and what we know about conventions is that while they can be very powerful, they can change and fall into decline. This means that any classification of classifications, any survey of styles, is at best a historical snapshot of some ways of achieving some effects so long as certain sociopolitical conditions—conditions that form expectations writers can use strategically—are in place. And that means that the categories I use to organize this book are, in a nonculpable sense, arbitrary, though they have not been chosen randomly. I believe them to be real and to correspond to choices writers might make; but I also believe that other categories could easily have been employed to good effect. Indeed, the list of sentence types is endless and is always being added to. New ways of doing things with language's limited but protean repertoire of forms are always being invented.

Here is a very partial classification of sentences, some of which will turn up in these pages, some of which won't. There are short sentences and long sentences, formal sentences and colloquial sentences, sentences that satisfy expectations and sentences that don't, sentences that go in a straight line and sentences that surprise, right-branching sentences and left-branching sentences, sentences that reassure and sentences that disturb, quiet sentences and sentences that explode like hand grenades, sentences that invite you in and sentences that exclude you, sentences that caress you and sentences that assault you, sentences that hide their art and sentences that ask readers to stand up and applaud. The language's resources are finite, but the effects that can be achieved by deploying them are not, and the skill of writing is to find those (formal) resources that will produce the effect you desire. Here is Edgar Allan Poe making the point in a question that should, he says, be in the forefront of every writer's mind at the beginning of the task:

> *Of the innumerable effects or impressions of which the heart, the intellect or (more generally) the soul is susceptible, what one shall I, on the present occasion, select?*
> ("The Philosophy of Composition," 1846)

In short, pick your effect, figure out what you want to do, and then figure out how to do it.

# CHAPTER 5

# THE SUBORDINATING STYLE

ALTHOUGH THERE ARE any number (an infinite number) of things you might want to do, effects you might want to achieve, two are general enough to serve as a basic classification and as a port of entry into the wonderful world of sentences. They are again formal categories; that is, one can distinguish between them without reference to content; but they are powerfully different and different in a way that has a content of its own. Let's call them the subordinating style and the additive style (they have different names in the technical literature). The subordinating style orders its components in relationships of causality (one event or state is caused by another), temporality (events and states are prior or subsequent to one another), and precedence (events and states are arranged in hierarchies of importance). "It was the books I read in high school rather than those I was assigned in college that influenced the choices I find myself making today"—two actions, one of which is prior to the other and has more significant effects that continue into the present. Contrast that sentence with this one: "I read *Hamlet*, and the entire semester was a drag and I learned how to fly." There might be some relationship between reading *Hamlet*, having a bad semester, and learning how to fly, but the sentence doesn't specify it; rather it just reports these events in a loose sequence, like beads on a string, without pressuring the reader to order or arrange them. That is the additive style (in one of its tamer versions). Each style has its beauties and its uses, and each typically projects a distinctive personality with a distinctive way of looking at the world. By choosing one or the other (they can of course be mixed and matched), a writer conveys something even before anything substantive has been said.

Suppose, for example, you want to communicate confidence in your assertions and suggest that no one could possibly be of any other opinion. You might write a subordinating sentence like the one that opens Jane Austen's *Pride and Prejudice*:

> *It is a truth universally acknowledged, that a single man in possession of a good fortune must be in want of a wife.*

In this sentence the claim of general truth is explicitly announced in the first clause, and the status of what follows it is established before it appears. But even if the sentence read: "A single man in possession of a good fortune must be in want of a wife," the effect would be achieved. The sentence would then divide in two, with "be"—a verb that declares something to be the case—as the hinge. The two clauses—"A man in possession of a good fortune" and "in want of a wife"—exhibit parallel structures: "a man in possession of" and "in want of." Possession of fortune is not enough; it must be completed, in the world and in the syntax, by the possession of a wife; "must be" does not invite dissent; it is the equivalent of "Who could think otherwise? Why else would a man have a fortune?" The relative brevity of the sentence is important in securing the effect; it suggests a portable truth that can be carried about and produced at any time. Sentences like this are rhythmic in feel and easy to remember; they can be delivered with a click and a snap. "A stitch in time saves nine." "A bird in the hand is worth two in the bush." "Out of sight, out of mind." "Power corrupts and absolute power corrupts absolutely." "Ask not what your country can do for you, ask what you can do for your country." "The road of excess leads to the palace of wisdom." "An apple a day keeps the doctor away." "Patriotism is the last refuge of a scoundrel."

The terms for this kind of sentence are many: aphorism, proverb, adage, dictum, apothegm, sententia, maxim. The name is less important than the form, which is the pithy pronouncement of wisdom in a manner that does not invite disagreement. Austen's sentence does not quite fit the pattern: it's a bit too long, and because attention is called to the absoluteness of the claim, that claim is ever so lightly undermined; "must be" in combination with "truth universally acknowledged" is a little bit too insistent and allows us to suspect an author mocking her own absolute pronouncement. It may seem counterintuitive, but you'll have a better chance of persuading readers that what you are about to say is universally acknowledged as a truth if you don't actually use the phrase "It is a truth universally acknowledged."

Just as you can practice writing three-word sentences or sentences that travel across time zones, so can you practice writing sentences that breathe unshakable conviction. Keep them short, employ parallel structures, use the present tense, limit yourself to relatively small words. "If you're waiting for fortune to smile, you may endure many a dark day." "Do your best, but expect the worst." "When someone rises to a point of principle, watch your back." "Politicians promise relief but give you grief." I made those up, and they're not very good; but I think I could get better, and if I did, I would become more skilled in the succinct presentation of wise sayings. At the same time, I would be forced to think about what a wise saying is and perhaps even to ponder the nature of wisdom. A discipline in form is a discipline in thought. There's an aphorism for you, and it may even be wise.

Sentences that package wisdom confidently always feel planned rather than spontaneous. Shorter sentences feel planned because they have the proverbial air of being prepackaged. The writer is saying, "I didn't make this up on the fly; I'm just giving form to what everyone knows." Longer sentences can achieve a similar effect by calling attention to their own construction. The writer is saying, "I'm not just putting down whatever comes into my head; I'm giving you the ordered fruits of my considered deliberations." Here, for example, is the opening sentence of Henry James's story "The Real Thing" (1892):

> *When the porter's wife (she used to answer the house-bell), announced "A gentleman—with a lady, sir," I had, as I often had in those days, for the wish was father to the thought, an immediate vision of sitters.*

Rather than putting the reader in direct contact with the event it describes, this sentence filters the event through layers of reflection. There is the reflection that comes along with framing the event in the past: "I had an immediate vision of sitters." (The speaker, we learn later, is a portrait painter.) The narrator reports on his thinking; he doesn't engage in it on the page. Before reporting on it, he gives it a history and a pedigree; it wasn't a spontaneous thought but one he had often ("as I often had in those days") and it is a thought that he generalizes into a type with an aphorism: "the wish was father to the thought." Because it is parenthetical, that aphorism delays the forward progress of the sentence; as the sentence pauses, the narrator seems to hover above it (this is a second layer of reflection), watching it unfold. The sentence's forward progress has already been delayed by the parenthetical clause "she used to answer the house-bell," a superfluous piece of information that serves only to push the perspective from which the "action" is observed further back into the past. These effects are frowned on by textbook writers who tell you (as Joseph Williams does in *Style: Ten Lessons in Clarity and Grace*, 1981) to avoid interrupting verbs and objects. The force of James's sentence depends on just such an interruption, which puts a screen between the reader and the immediacy that might be the goal of another writer who was trying to impart information succinctly or issue orders with the force of a command or pass down a recipe.

You can learn to write sentences like James's. You start with a kernel assertion, say, "the door opened." And then you back up in time to a prior action or event presented in what is called a dependent clause: "As he reached the crest of the hill and saw the house with its imposing spires." Throw in a bit of parenthetical meta-reflection: "—they looked like spears ready to impale him—"; and then slow down the concluding assertion: "the door, moving it seemed under its own power, opened." And then you have it. "As he reached the crest of the hill and saw the house with its imposing spires—they looked like spears ready to impale him—the door, moving it seemed under its own power, opened." Not James by any means, but a passable cheap imitation.

Once you've done it a few times, you can produce sentences like this forever. The skill is no different from the skill involved in turning three-word sentences into one-hundred-word monsters. It's just that instead of trying to cram as much as you can into the spaces between the words, you're trying to embed propositions in complex logical structures. Most of all you are practicing subordination, the art of arranging objects and actions in relationships of causality, temporality, and precedence. It is one thing to say, "x is the case," and then to say, "before x was y," and then to say, "x caused y," and then to say, "linking x and y was z," and then to say, "x is more significant than y." It is another thing to say all of these in a single syntactic unit that breathes design and control. (This distinction does not imply a judgment of superiority; as we shall see, the additive style—one assertion after another—can be as artful as the style that embeds.)

The technical term for the accomplishment of the subordinating style is hypotaxis, defined by Richard Lanham as "an arrangement of clauses or phrases in a dependent or subordinate relationship" (*A Handlist of Rhetorical Terms*, 1991). Hypotaxis, Lanham explains, "lets us know how things rank, what derives from what" (*Analyzing Prose*, 1993). (The fact that "hypotaxis" is a Greek word tells you how old the classification of styles is.) The James sentence is a modest version of the style. More elaborate versions can go on forever, piling up clauses and suspending completion in a way that creates a desire for completion and an incredible force when completion finally occurs.

Near the end of Herman Melville's *Billy Budd, Sailor* (1891, 1924), the hanging of the title figure is presented in a sentence that delays the event by filling in its circumstances. As a result, when it finally occurs, it has been freighted with layers of meaning:

> *At the same moment, it chanced that the vapory fleece*
> *hanging low in the East was shot through with a soft*
> *glory as of the fleece of the Lamb of God seen in mysti-*
> *cal vision, and simultaneously therewith, watched by*
> *the wedged mass of upturned faces, Billy ascended, and,*
> *ascending, took the full rose of the dawn.*

The action of the sentence and its main clause are simple: "Billy ascended." But he ascends in the context of allusions to both the Annunciation—the upturned faces play the role of the shepherds—and the Crucifixion. By the time he acts, Billy is both sacrifice and savior, the slain lamb and the lamb whose blood redeems; he is the centerpiece of what the sentence describes as a "mystical vision." Because we have been made to wait for the filling in of the vision, which comes complete with viewers of what might almost be a large Renaissance painting, the moment of ascension seems static and staged; motion is stopped. But the "and" that follows "ascended" functions as a release—we experience it as a pregnant pause—and the present participle "ascending" initiates an upward movement syntactically, visually, and thematically. (One hears an echo, perhaps, of lines 11 and 12 of Shakespeare's Sonnet 29: "Like to the lark at break of day arising / From sullen earth, sings hymns at heaven's gate.") Like the gaze of the "upturned faces," our gaze soars upward, missing entirely the pain of the hanging; and the sentence misses it too, coming to rest where Billy rests, in the glory of the full rose (a pun on "rise"?) of dawn. He is risen.

Where in Melville's sentence the clauses preceding the main event lean backward, in this famous sentence from Martin Luther King Jr.'s *Letter from a Birmingham Jail* (1963), they lean forward, straining to get where you know long before the end they are going to go:

> . . . *when you have seen vicious mobs lynch your mothers and fathers at will and drown your sisters and brothers at*

*whim; when you have seen hate-filled policemen curse, kick, brutalize and even kill your black brothers and sisters with impunity; when you see the vast majority of your twenty million Negro brothers smothering in an airtight cage of poverty in the midst of an affluent society; when you suddenly find your tongue twisted and your speech stammering as you seek to explain to your six-year-old daughter why she can't go to the public amusement park that has just advertised on television, and see tears welling up in her little eyes when she is told that Funtown is closed to colored children, and see the depressing clouds of inferiority beginning to form in her little mental sky, and see her beginning to distort her personality by developing a bitterness toward white people; when you have to concoct an answer for a five-year-old son asking in agonizing pathos: "Daddy, why do white people treat colored people so mean?"; when you take a cross-country drive and find it necessary to sleep night after night in the uncomfortable corners of your automobile because no motel will accept you; when you are humiliated day in and day out by nagging signs reading "white" and "colored"; when your first name becomes "nigger," your middle name becomes "boy" (however old you are) and your last name becomes "John," and your wife and mother are never given the respected title "Mrs."; when you are harried by day and haunted by night by the fact that you are a Negro, living constantly at tiptoe stance never quite knowing what to expect next, and are plagued with inner fears and outer resentments; when you are forever fighting a degenerating sense of "nobodiness"; then you will understand why we find it difficult to wait.*

King is replying to the question (sometimes asked by his colleagues in the movement) "Why don't you wait a while and hold back on the sit-ins and marches?" The answer is at once withheld and given. It is formally withheld by the succession of "when" clauses (the technical name is anaphora), that offer themselves as preliminary to the direct assertion but *are* the direct assertion; each "when" clause is presented as a piece of the answer, but is in itself fully sufficient as an answer. "Here is the reason we can't wait," each says, but if that isn't enough, here is another and another. As the huge dependent clause (a clause that does not stand alone as a complete sentence) grows and grows, the independent clause—the sentence's supposedly main assertion—becomes less and less necessary. Meanwhile, there is an incredible amount of cross-referencing and rhetorical counterpointing going on among the clauses as they advance inexorably toward the waiting, and foreknown, conclusion. A full explication of these inter-clause effects would require an essay. It would include an analysis of the rhyming pattern of "will," "whim," and "kill," which links and bookends the pairs "mothers and fathers," "sisters and brothers," and "brothers and sisters." It would include an analysis of the interplay between inner and outer that begins with the phrase "ominous clouds of inferiority," continues with "her little mental sky," and reaches a climax with King's acknowledgment of "inner fears" that at once reflect and war with "outer resentments." It would include an analysis of the progression from "nigger" to "boy" to "John" in counterpoint with the withheld honorific "Mrs." and ending with the word "Negro," which does not quite reclaim the dignity history has taken from it. But it is enough to note the main effect: the building of intolerable pressure as the succession of "when" clauses details the layered humiliations every black man, woman, and child suffers, and then the spectacularly understated, even quiet, anticlimactic conclusion "then you will understand why we find it difficult to wait."

It is a tremendous rhetorical achievement, a sentence for the ages, but again you can learn how to imitate it, if not to match it. Pick any topic, even a trivial one, say, getting up in the morning in the face of all the reasons not to: "When you've stayed up all night watching *Rocky* for the twentieth time, when the temperature is below freezing and you're warm underneath the blanket, when the day promises only drudgery and humiliation, when the conclusion that your life has been for naught and no one will miss you seems self-evident, when everyone you have ever cared for is either dead or angry with you, when the only pleasure you can anticipate is a cup of coffee you can barely afford, when the thought of one more day doing something you absolutely hate is unbearable, then you remind yourself of what Scarlett O'Hara said: 'Tomorrow is another day.'" The sentence is bathetic, even pathetic, but its form is the same as the form of King's sentence, and if you learn how to master the form, you can employ it "naturally" when you have something important to say.

King's sentence has affinities with what is known in the history of style as the Ciceronian period, a "long stately sentence which suspends the verb until the end . . . with chains of subordinate clauses and balanced antitheses" (John R. Holmes, *Encyclopedia of the Essay*, 1997). Michael Sheehan offers as an example these lines from *Hamlet*. The speaker is

Claudius, the brother of the hero's murdered father: "Therefore our sometime sister, now our queen / Th'imperial jointress to this warlike state, / Have we, as 'twere with a defeated joy, / . . . With mirth in funeral, and with dirge in marriage, / In equal scale weighing delight and dole, / Taken to wife" (Wordmall: A Blog About the English Language, 2006). Or, in short, I've married my brother's widow shortly after his death. By delaying the verb, Claudius is able to provide his own analysis of the action he takes before he names it. He confronts the stigma against marrying one's sister-in-law (see Leviticus 20:21) directly: once our sister, now our queen; he reminds his hearers that because she is his queen, she is theirs and a partner to his military power; he acknowledges the doubleness and dubiousness of the act with a series of paradoxical antitheses: defeated joy, mirth in funeral, dirge in marriage, delight and dole; he claims to have carefully considered what he is going to do ("In equal scale weighing"), and then, after all this buildup, he springs the simple, but not all that simple, fact of what he has already done: "Taken to wife."

One scholar explains that the characteristic effects of this style were achieved by advance planning: "one knew from the outset of a period where it was going and how it was going to get there" (Jonas Barish, *Ben Jonson and the Language of Prose Comedy*, 1960). This describes the achievement from the perspective of the writer. The reader, however, doesn't know where the writer is going; he knows only that the person taking him there is in control. Control is what this style at once performs and announces, and no one does it better than John Milton. At a moment in his pamphlet *An Apology Against a Pamphlet* (1642), Milton rejects the praise of his writing style offered by an adversary and pushes away artfulness in a sentence that could hardly be more artful:

> *For me, readers, although I cannot say that I am utterly untrained in those rules which best rhetoricians have given, or unacquainted with those examples which the prime authors of eloquence have written in any learned tongue, yet true eloquence I find to be none but the serious and hearty love of truth, and that whose mind so ever is fully possessed with a fervent desire to know good things and with the dearest charity to infuse the knowledge of them into others, when such a man would speak, his words (by what I can express), like so many nimble and airy servitors, trip about him at command, and in well ordered files, as he would wish, fall aptly into their own places.*

The basic structure of the sentence is "although . . . yet." The "although" clause typically gives reasons why the statement or resolution in the "yet" clause is somewhat of a surprise or even a non sequitur. "Although I hate and fear this kind of situation, yet I'll come with you." "Although I don't know what I'm doing, yet I'm going ahead." (This is another formal structure that can be played with infinitely.) In Milton's sentence the negative proposition that is supposed to throw the positive resolution "yet I can speak well" into relief is "I have no training in the arts of eloquence": "Although I have no training in the arts of eloquence, yet I can speak well from the heart." If the heart and the intention are good, the words will follow without the need of any rhetorical exertions. But Milton is playing rhetorical tricks from the beginning, and their effect is to take back the concession of the "although" clause even as it is being offered. "I cannot say that I am utterly untrained" neither claims nor disclaims training. "Utterly" is particularly coy. It says, well, I may have a little training, maybe even a lot. The phrase "or unacquainted with those examples" further undermines the supposed self-deprecation—yeah, I may have studied some of those virtuoso rhetoricians in many languages—and endows the speaker with the very credentials he is pooh-poohing. It's as if a movie star were to get up and say, "Although I have only won four Academy Awards, yet I still have a modest talent to offer you." So that when Milton gets to the hinge of his sentence—"yet true eloquence I find"—we are more than prepared for the self-praise that follows. He is obviously the one who is possessed by virtue and the desire to infuse it into others; it is his portrait that is being painted; he is "such a man" ("When such a man would speak"), and the false modesty of "by what I can express" is almost offensive. It is an "Emperor's New Clothes" strategy in reverse: Milton is asking us to see him as rhetorically naked (just plain old virtuous me, folks) at the moment when he completes a rhetorical triumph, the moment when his words perform exactly the action they are reporting, tripping about at his command. This is a textbook example of imitative form (sometimes called a fallacy, but it is not): Milton's words do what they describe; they fall aptly in their own places just as those very words are being intoned. The note of triumph is unmistakable; the request for applause palpable and difficult to resist.

Milton's sentence celebrates an inner virtue that resists and masters the apparent flux of temporal life. In the conclusion to *The Renaissance* (1873),Walter Pater makes the opposite point—there is only flux; perdurability is an illusion—but he conveys it in prose that is as controlled and controlling as Milton's. Pater has been explaining that the impressions that make up our experience are momentary and that each of them is "infinitively divisible" into smaller impressions that are themselves infinitely divisible. Then comes the sentence that matches Milton's in the artfulness with which it enacts what it describes:

> *To such a tremulous wisp constantly re-forming itself on the stream, to a single sharp impression, with a sense in it, a relic more or less fleeting, of such moments gone by, what is real in our lives fines itself down.*

In this sentence the main assertion—"what is real in our lives fines itself down"—is again delayed by a series of clauses laid side by side, and these clauses take away in advance what the independent clause promises: a stable reality. The reader is repeatedly teased with a stability of reference that barely survives the moment of its (fleeting) appearance. In the first clause the (relative) stability is compromised before it appears. A wisp is already a "fleeting trace" (*American Heritage Dictionary*), but it is preceded in the sentence by "tremulous"; so what we have (or don't have) is a trace of something we know not what, and that trace is itself quivering and escaping from our grasp. The next word, "constantly," mocks us with the root "constant"—steadfast—but the constancy asserted is the constancy of continually "re-forming"—that is, always in the process of becoming something else; and even that process is occurring in and on a fluid medium, itself always re-forming "on the stream." The next clause brings a word that promises to arrest the flux—"sharp"—but the noun it modifies is "impression"; and then we are told that we don't even have the impression, only a "sense" of it (an impression of an impression), and that sense is itself a "relic" (a trace again) and that relic of a sense of an impression is "fleeting"; "more or less" does not allow us even to fasten on "fleeing." The sentence's summary statement affords us the temporary ease of the word "moments," but immediately those moments are said to be "gone by"—now you see them, now you never did. The sentence's final tease is the phrase "real in our lives," which names everything that has been taken away. The phrase shines there for an instant before it is refined ("fines") into something that will then refine itself ad infinitum "down" into the ever-receding world of fleeting, dissolving, infinitely divisible impressions.

When the sentence is over, nothing is left but itself. Like Shelley's "Ozymandias" and George Herbert's "Church Monuments," it scoffs at monumentality but is itself a monument. Although Pater and Milton proclaim antithetical messages in their sentences—one insisting on a unitary abiding truth, the other announcing that nothing abides—the two sentences are rhetorically similar: each leads the reader down a path that lies waiting for him or her; each says, in addition to the substantive things it says, you are in the company of a mind that has thought it all out and is delivering it to you with complete mastery.

# CHAPTER 6

# THE ADDITIVE STYLE

SENTENCES LIKE MILTON'S and Pater's are not bashful about foregrounding the process of their own construction. They flaunt their artfulness and invite readers to share in the verbal pyrotechnics they display. But suppose you wanted to achieve another effect, the effect not of planning, order, and control, but of spontaneity, haphazardness, and chance. Then you might avail yourself of another style, no less artful, but marked by the appearance of artlessness. The fountain of this style is the French essayist Michel de Montaigne (1533–1592), who announces (in "A Consideration Upon Cicero"), "I write naturally and without a plan; the first stroke of the pen just leads to a second." (*Je commence volontiers sans project; le premier trait produit le second.*) Montaigne's claim is to be expressing himself without premeditation or rhetorical design (Milton's claim, but Montaigne actually means it): "I do not portray [finished] being; I portray passing . . . from day to day, minute to minute . . . This is a record of various and changeable occurrences, and of irresolute and, when it so befalls, contradictory ideas" ("Of Repentance"). The word "essay" means to try out, test, probe. In the essay style, successive clauses and sentences are not produced by an overarching logic, but by association; the impression the prose gives is that it can go anywhere in a manner wholly unpredictable. Rather than indicating the logical progression of thought, connectives such as "thus" and "so" are just place markers; "but" and "and" are the words that carry the experience forward, the first signaling a thought going in a new direction, the second saying "and, oh, this has just occurred to me." The technical name for the style is parataxis: "a coordinate, rather than a subordinate, construction." (Don't worry about the term; you don't have to learn it, but it might be useful at a cocktail party.) The units of this kind of prose, explains historian of style Morris Croll, are "connected with each other by only the slightest of ligatures, each one carrying a stronger emphasis . . . than it would have if it were more strictly subordinated" (*Style, Rhetoric and Rhythm*, 1966). Montaigne's translator Donald Frame sums up the style and its effect: "Free, oral, informal, personal, concrete . . . spontaneous in order, ranging from the epigrammatic to the ambling and associative. It communicates the flavor of the man" (*The Complete Essays of Montaigne*).

Or so is the claim. Montaigne may have believed that a style that eschews formal structure and obvious design accurately mirrors the movements of a mind (his own) in free-flowing motion; but the "natural" style is a style nevertheless, not a transparent picture of psychological reality, but a representation of it, neither more nor less "true" than the representation of thought offered by the deliberative, subordinating style. There is certainly a difference between saying in response to the perennial question "What did you do today?" "I had five distinct experiences that seemed unconnected but were related in the following ways," and saying, "Well, I got up and made coffee; and do you remember the day we bought the coffeemaker in that little shop; let's go back there soon; and, oh yes, I went to the grocery store; they're so rude, we really should find someplace else; and you'll never guess who I met there—Sheila; and she told me that . . ." But it is a difference between ways of organizing experience, not a difference between a filtered experience and the thing itself.

It is also a difference between the experience the styles provide. Readers of Austen, James, Melville, Pater, and Milton will feel secure (if a bit condescended to) in the hands of a controlling intelligence who guides them with authority through the intricacies of a densely layered but finely ordered piece of prose. Readers of authors less intent on being seen as holding the reins will experience a degree of the same freedom, looseness, and, on occasion, disorientation the prose seems to be enacting. (Remember, it's all art.) Here are two examples from the famous openings of two famous books, Laurence Sterne's *Tristram Shandy* (1759–1766) and J. D. Salinger's *Catcher in the Rye* (1951).

*Tristram Shandy* begins with our hero recounting a

moment he could not possibly remember, the moment of his conception:

> *I wish either my father or my mother, or indeed both of them, as they were in duty both equally bound to it, had minded what they were about when they begot me; had they duly considered how much depended upon what they were doing—that not only the production of a rational Being was concerned in it, but that possibly the happy formation and temperature of his body, perhaps his genius and the very cast of his mind; and for aught they knew to the contrary, even the fortunes of his whole house might take their turn from the humours and dispositions which were then uppermost—had they duly weighed and considered all this, and proceeded accordingly—I am verily persuaded I should have made a different figure in the world from that in which the reader is likely to see me.*

No preliminaries or ceremony here. The speaker just bursts upon our stage, wishing and revising his wish as he goes. First it is "either" his mother or father who is the object of his reproach; then he bethinks himself and says no, actually both; and then he gives the reason for his self-correction; they were after all equal partners in the act whose possible consequences are then rehearsed in a list that could have gone on forever. One thought leads to another and then to another, each provisional and not quite followed through, until, in an act of will—there is no natural stopping place—the speaker puts a (temporary) period to his musings by revealing the wish behind his wish: I might have been a different person than the one you now see.

But we don't see him at all; what we see is an always receding "figure" whom we proceed to chase through the many pages that follow. Early and famous reviewers (Edmund Burke, William Hazlitt, Sir Walter Scott) called Sterne's style careless, haphazard, shifting, rambling, and conversational, "a book without plan or order" (Walter Bagehot). There were complaints that nothing quite got finished. The author, Burke observed, "perpetually digresses; or rather having no determined end in view, he runs from object to object, as they happen to strike a very lively and irregular imagination." In the end—there is no end—"the book is a perpetual series of disappointments." A twentieth-century commentator (Lodwick Hartley) gets the style and its effect exactly right when he asks, "Who can tolerate the person who in ordinary conversation is forever backing and filling, embroidering and elaborating, detailing and digressing in a such a way as never to get his story told?" (*Laurence Sterne's Tristram Shandy: A Norton Critical Edition*). Of course this is not ordinary conversation, but planned conversation designed to appear ordinary in an extraordinary way. The expectations Sterne's prose repeatedly disappoints are the expectations that come along with a belief in a rationally ordered universe, a belief that is conveyed, even breathed, by the subordinating linear style we have seen in writers like Austen, James, Milton, Melville, and Martin Luther King Jr. In place of the unity and coherence attempted and achieved by these authors, Sterne puts "a seemingly new pattern of unity; not new but as old as humanity: the organic pattern of life" (Toby A. Olshin, in *Laurence Sterne's Tristram Shandy: A Norton Critical Edition*).

The organic pattern of life does not develop; it just grows, and representations of it often frustrate those who want to travel a straight line from the beginning to the middle to the end of a sentence, or of anything else. Sterne's Tristram is well aware of his readers' desires, and he comments on them even as he refuses to satisfy them. "I know there are readers in the world . . . who are no readers at all—who find themselves ill at ease, unless they are let into the whole secret from first to last, of every thing which concerns you." They are not readers at all because they are not trying to put things together or figure them out (two meanings of the verb "to read"); rather, they want it all to be given to them nicely tied up in a neat package. It is those (non)readers he aims to tease when he tells them what he won't tell them: "Sir, as you and I are in a manner perfect strangers to each other, it would not have been proper to have let you into too many circumstances relating to myself all at once—you must have a little patience." That is a straightforward sentence, but the Shandean style returns immediately, imitating what it urges:

> *Therefore my dear friend and companion, if you should think me somewhat sparing of my narrative on my first setting out—bear with me—and let me go on, and tell my story my own way—or if I should seem now and then to trifle upon the road—or should sometime put on a fool's cap with a bell to it, for a moment or two as we pass along—don't fly off—but rather courteously give me credit*

*for a little more wisdom than appears upon my outside—*
*and as we jog along, either laugh with me, or at me, or in*
*short, do any thing—only keep your temper.*

Let me go on, he says, as he goes on, and drags us with him. The work of the sentence is done by those loose connectives "and," "or," and "but," each of which signals a new turn or detour and all of which conspire to keep the reader—mockingly referred to as "my dear friend and companion"—off-balance. The message is either keep up with me or keep quiet.

J. D. Salinger's Holden Caulfield does not even pretend to be solicitous of his reader. His opening sentence announces that whatever the reader might want, he's not going to get it. Holden refuses to begin at the beginning and "tell you my whole goddamn autobiography or anything." (The dismissiveness of "or anything" is a thing of insolent beauty.)

*If you really want to hear about it, the first thing you'll*
*probably want to know is where I was born, and what*
*my lousy childhood was like, and how my parents were*
*occupied and all before they had me, and all that David*
*Copperfield kind of crap, but I don't feel like going into it,*
*if you want to know the truth.*

The sentence lists the information it won't provide, stringing the items it will withhold on a bead of ands—none of that and none of that and none of that either. The art of the sentence consists in its ability to convey two voices: the breathless, unrehearsed voice of the teenager and the reflective, quasi-philosophical voice of the author. When Holden throws out "lousy" he intends nothing more than a contemptuous filler (today a teenage narrator might say "f★★★★★★"), but Salinger wants to raise the questions of just what kind of childhood his young hero had. In Holden's mind, "if you want to know the truth" is a throwaway that means "I don't care what you want," but Salinger is telling us that the truth of his novel will not be the *David Copperfield* kind ("To begin my life with the beginning of my life, I record that I was born [as I have been informed and believe] on a Friday, at twelve o'clock at night"). It will be something else, and that something else will not be revealed by dates and orderly sequences.

*Catcher in the Rye* not only exhibits but is about the continuous and unpredictable stream of experience in relation to which clean, formal demarcations, either in life or in prose, are artificial impositions. Later in the book, Holden recalls why he flunked Oral Expression; he couldn't stomach the instructor's insistence that speakers not digress from a stated point. "The trouble with me is, I *like* it when somebody digresses," and he illustrates his preferred style of speaking (and thinking) with the speech of a boy who got a D-plus because he said he was going to talk about his father's farm, but then:

> *What he did was, Richard Kinsella, he'd start telling you all about that stuff—then all of a sudden he'd start telling you about this letter his mother got from his uncle, and how his uncle got polio and all when he was forty-two years old, how he wouldn't let anybody come to see him in the hospital because he didn't want anybody to see him with a brace on.*

Richard's style is associative, as is the style of the sentence that recalls his performance and mimes it. "Then," "all of a sudden," "how"—these are classic paratactic connectives; they just get you from one piece of prose to the next without insisting on the priority or superior importance of any of them. Holden pronounces the effect "*nice*" and elaborates: "It's nice when somebody tells you about their uncle. Especially when they start out telling you about their father's farm, and then all of a sudden get more interested in their uncle." Just go with the flow, either in life or in writing; don't stop to put events and objects in ordered relationships to one another.

The great modern theorist of the additive, or coordinating, style is Gertrude Stein, who explains in an amazing sentence why she doesn't employ punctuation that carves reality into manageable units of completed and organized thought:

> When I first began writing I felt that writing should go on
> I still do feel that it should go on but when I first began
> writing I was completely possessed by the necessity that
> writing should go on and if writing should go on what had
> colons and semi-colons to do with it, what had commas to
> do with it what had periods to do with it what had small
> letters and capitals to do with it to do with writing going
> on which was at the time the most profound need I had in
> connection with writing.
>
> (*Lectures in America*, 1935)

Colons, commas, periods, and capital letters segment a

reality that is continuous and made up of discrete, intensely realized moments. Immediacy, not linear reflection leading to a conclusion, is the goal here, and to reach it Stein must at once write sentences and somehow defeat the deferral of meaning—the sense of building toward a completed thought—that is the very nature of a sentence. Usually a sentence does not deliver its meaning until the end, and only at the end do its components acquire their significance and weight. But what Stein wants is meaning to be present at every instant, to be always the same in weight and yet different as each word is different. Before Flaubert and Cézanne, she explains, "composition had consisted of a central idea to which everything else was an accompaniment and separate but was not an end in itself." But then "Cézanne conceived the idea that in composition one thing was as important as another thing. Each part is as important as the whole, and it impressed me enormously," and as a consequence, she continues, "I tried to convey the idea of each part of a composition being as important as the whole" ("A Transatlantic Interview," 1946). Indeed, it is composition itself—arranging elements in a linear design—that is the enemy of this effort in Stein's eyes: "Everything is the same except composition and time" ("Composition as Explanation," 1926), that is, before composition—putting things together to form a larger whole—spoils it by relating and subordinating.

The insight is theological, although Stein probably doesn't intend it that way. In a world created and presided over by an omnipresent God who fills all the available spaces, the distinctions between things, persons, and events are illusory, a function of a partial, divided, and dividing consciousness. The seventeenth-century English poet George Herbert says it succinctly: "We say amiss / This or that is, / Thy word is all if we could spell" ("The Flower"). If we would only stop spelling, stop laboring to put discrete significances together in an effort to combine them into a larger whole, we could see, theologians tell us, that the larger whole we seek is already everywhere and that our very efforts to apprehend it themselves signify it. But this would mean giving up or letting go of consecutive thought, of the impulse to predication and sentence making. And how in the world (a phrase meant literally) could we do that? It is impossible. Nevertheless, that impossibility is pretty much Stein's project. I was groping, she says, "toward a continuous present, a using everything a beginning again and again and then everything being alike then everything very simply everything was naturally simply different and so I as a contemporary was creating everything being alike was creating everything naturally being naturally simply different, everything being alike" ("Composition as Explanation"). In this sentence likeness and difference, the basic constituents of a discourse that anatomizes and ranks, change places, go in opposite directions, come together again, are in the end made one. By insisting on the alikeness in value of every word, Stein also insists on the difference or uniqueness of every word. "I took individual words and thought about them until I got their weight and volume complete and put them next to another word" ("A Transatlantic Interview"). The result is sentences that circle around again and again to words that simultaneously stand alone and take their place in the ongoingness that is at once proclaimed—"writing should go on"—and enacted.

The very word "sentence" means a finished thought, a verdict, a judgment, a piece of wisdom—all of which meanings Stein's prose refuses in a brilliant effort to make language perform (these are her words) "like a cinema picture made up of succession and each moment having its own emphasis that is its own difference, and so there was the moving and the existence of each moment as it was in me" ("Portraits and Repetition"). She wanted, she says, "the pleasure of concentrating on the final simplicity of excessive complication." If the complication of a sentence was less than excessive, the prose would stop on a single point and not be ongoing. She wanted to defeat subordination. "A long complicated sentence should force itself upon you, make you know yourself knowing it" (*Lectures in America*). The difficulty of negotiating such a sentence has as its reward both the knowledge composition will obscure—the knowledge of words and things before they are subordinated to some "central idea"—and the knowledge of that in you which desires the wrapped-up closure a Stein sentence will not deliver. The trick, Stein explains, is to have "done something that was not leading to anything."

Now, doing something that is not leading to anything would seem to be a description of the kinds of sentences I was saying at the beginning you shouldn't write because they degenerate into lists and fragments. If a sentence is a structure of logical relationships—the mantra I urged on you only a short while ago—what exactly is a sequence of words that, like Stein's, pushes logic and coherent, consecutive thought away?

At its furthest reaches the additive style may achieve a degree of looseness, of associative nonconnectedness that is radically antithetical to sentence making, at least as I have wanted you to understand it. I raise the issue, but I will put off taking it up until we have a few more examples on the table.

Stein was an acknowledged influence on another master of the coordinating style, Ernest Hemingway. But Hemingway's views on writing were less philosophical than hers and stemmed mainly from his early career as a journalist. Hence his famous pieces of advice to writers: use short sentences, write clearly, use simple Anglo-Saxon words, don't overwrite, avoid adjectives (a lesson he learned from Ezra Pound), and leave yourself out of it. The result was a style that has been described as realistic, hardboiled, spare, unadorned, minimalist, and lapidary. The last two words are particularly apt: a lapidary style is polished and cut to the point of transparency. It doesn't seem to be doing much. It does not demand that attention be paid to it. It aspires to a self-effacement that allows the object to shine through as a master stonecutter allows the beauty of the stone to shine through by paring away layers of it. Hemingway's sentences, unlike Stein's, do not "force themselves upon you." There is no "excessive complication." There is no complication at all, just (or so is the claim) the thing itself, limpidly presented.

Here, for example, is the second sentence of *A Farewell to Arms* (1929):

> *In the bed of the river there were pebbles and boulders, dry and white in the sun, and the water was clear and swiftly moving and blue in the channels.*

The sentence divides in half, with the pebbles and boulders occupying one half and the water occupying the other half. No relationship between the two halves is explicitly asserted. They are just laid down next to each other, linked by an "and" that does minimal work. The clause "dry and white in the sun" is technically adjectival, but "dry" and "white" come across more as qualities (dryness and whiteness) than as modifiers. The water in the second half is a surrogate for the style's (unvoiced) claim to be making no claim for itself at all. Like the water, the style is "clear" and "swiftly moving"; it does not stop or take a turn or qualify something it has presented. In short, this "simple" sentence is an allegory—one of the most complex of literary forms—of its own unfolding.

Sentences like this one are employed by Hemingway as a contrast to the anguish, despair, and pointlessness often experienced by his characters. In *To Have and Have Not* (1937), Marie Morgan thinks about what life will be like now that her husband, Harry, has been killed. We overhear her inner monologue, written in a style that is almost a parody of Stein's; its repetitions, rather than circling around each other and straining toward a final complicating simplicity, are just . . . well, repetitions.

> *I guess you find out everything in this goddamned life. I*
> *guess you do all right. I guess I'm probably finding out*
> *right now. You just go dead inside and everything is easy.*
> *You just get dead like most people are most of the time.*
> *I guess that's how it is all right. I guess that's just about*
> *what happens to you. Well, I've got a good start. I've got*

*a good start if that's what you have to do. I guess that's*
*what you have to do all right. I guess that's it. I guess*
*that's what it comes to. All right. I got a good start then.*
*I'm way ahead of everybody now.*

This doesn't quite work, but you know what Hemingway
had in mind: he wanted to convey a consciousness in the process
of distilling a little bit of stoic hope out of a huge sea of troubles.
He succeeds in the next sentence by leaving human consciousness behind and moving to the only real realm of security and
stability, a landscape purged of human losses and perturbations:

*Outside it was a lovely, cool, subtropical winter day and*
*the palm branches were sawing in the light north wind.*

"Outside" is very precise; it means not inside, not inside the
mind of Marie or anyone else. "[L]ovely" and "cool" are attributes of natural phenomena that know nothing of the effect
they have on mortal agents. One is reminded both of the pas-
toral tradition in which Nature is often presented as indifferent
to man's woes and of William Carlos Williams's "The Red
Wheelbarrow," "glazed with rain water / beside the white
chickens," and declared to be more important than any human
perspective. Even when, in the novel's last sentence, the landscape contains objects that must be man-powered, those objects
have achieved the "thingness" and serenity of palm branches:

*A large white yacht was coming into the harbor and seven*
*miles out on the horizon you could see a tanker, small and*

*neat in profile against the blue sea, hugging the reef as she
made to the westward to keep from wasting fuel against
the stream.*

Three objects—the yacht, the tanker, and the sea—fill a
palette of white and blue. The yacht and the tanker are not
related to each other except as objects within the sentence's
pictorial frame. One is coming in to the observer, the other
moving away at a westward angle; both seem self-propelled. In
another sentence, "hugging" and "she" might be humanizing
touches; here they function as painterly details: the small and
neat boat stays close to the shore; it doesn't make love to it; the
feminine pronoun is merely precise, a feature of a language
that, like French, but less formally, classes things by gender
categories. It's sexuality without the sex, a peaceful realm of
nonaffect available to Hemingway's characters only in death.
Even the tension between the vessel and the currents of the sea
is muted and stilled as the tanker moves in a way calculated to
lessen it. In the same way, the tendency of language to move
to a point of judgment and discrimination is also stilled by a
syntax that refuses to develop or subordinate, and is held together by a slight connective ("and") and a present participle
("hugging") that is the declaration and vehicle of ongoingness.

Sterne, Salinger, Stein, Hemingway—the additive, non-
subordinating style is obviously versatile; it can be the vehicle
of comedy, social satire, philosophical reflection, realism, and
something approaching photography. In any of its guises it
displays the advantages of being able to stop on a dime, arrest
action, freeze the frame, stay still at the same time the reader

moves linearly—all effects achieved in spectacular fashion in a sentence from Virginia Woolf's *To the Lighthouse* (1927). Mrs. Ramsey has just rebuked her daughters for mocking "the little atheist" Tansley. We see them react in a moment that expands and remains in focus despite the passing of considerable reading time:

> *She was now formidable to behold, and it was only in*
> *silence, looking up from their plates, after she had spoken*
> *so severely about Charles Tansley, that her daughters,*
> *Prue, Nancy, Rose—could sport with infidel ideas which*
> *they had brewed for themselves of a life different from*
> *hers: in Paris, perhaps; a wilder life; not always taking*
> *care of some man or other; for there was in all their minds*
> *a mute questioning of deference and chivalry, of the Bank*
> *of England and the Indian Empire, of ringed fingers and*
> *lace, though to them all there was something in this of*
> *the essence of beauty, which called out the manliness in*
> *their girlish hearts, and made them, as they sat at table*
> *beneath their mother's eyes, honour her strange severity,*
> *her extreme courtesy, like a queen's raising from the*
> *mud a beggar's dirty foot and washing it, when she thus*
> *admonished them so severely about that wretched atheist*
> *who had chased them to—or, speaking accurately, been*
> *invited to stay with them in—the Isles of Skye.*

The word "behold" is a command: behold this woman! In the sentence, our surrogate beholders are the three daughters who gaze upward at their mother as if at a portrait and think thoughts in silence. From its beginning to "a life different from hers," the sentence proceeds in the subordinating, hypotactic mode: "looking up from their place" is the present action the three young woman perform, but the present is immediately framed by the "after" clause—"after she had spoken so severely"—which provides a past and causal perspective on what they are doing. But then, "in Paris, perhaps" the prose breaks free. Who says "perhaps"? Is it a qualification from the outside, made by an omniscient narrator, or does the word belong to the three sisters, who perhaps have not yet settled on their preferred dream? And who is it that wants not to be "always taking care of some man or other"? Surely the daughters have not yet taken on that burden; does this wish belong to their mother, who is now playing in the fields of her daughters' consciousnesses? Are the "infidel ideas" the sisters "sport" with theirs or hers? Is it for her or for themselves that they imagine "a life different" from the one their mother leads? The latter is the more likely; the austere majesty of Mrs. Ramsey leads them to question the world of ceremony and courtesy they associate with her; and yet—the sentence does not progress, but keeps adding to the perspectives and vistas that open up in its leisurely spaces—the severity from which they imagine themselves freed has its own attractions, its own beauty, which is summed up in the person of their mother, to whom they, and the sentence, return, re-conceiving her as a queen admonishing her subjects. At the same moment the subordinating style, with its clear temporal demarcations ("who had chased them—or, speaking accurately, been invited to stay with them"), also returns, putting events and persons in their proper place.

What makes the Woolf sentence able to shift direction and emphases without seeming discontinuous or disjointed are those "slight ligatures" that mark the coordinating style: "and," "for," "though," "when." These interact with a succession of present participles—"looking," "taking," "raising," "speaking"—verbal forms indicating ongoing actions, no one of which is completed and all of which combine in almost a symphonic fashion to paint a densely layered moving, kaleidoscopic, sometimes frame-frozen picture.

Earlier I remarked that sentence makers are selectors; possibilities must be foreclosed so that clear and demarcated relationships can come into sharp view. But it is just such a discipline that the additive writer refuses, cultivating a looseness that allows meaning and worlds to enter and leave freely. Like Stein, Woolf explicitly theorizes her method. Words, she says in "Craftsmanship" (1937), do not "express one simple statement but a thousand possibilities." Those possibilities are locked in as long as words are asked only to be useful; but liberate them from usefulness, and marvelous things happen. She illustrates by riffing on the words written on a sign in a railway carriage: "Do not lean out of the window":

> At the first reading, the useful meaning, the surface meaning, is conveyed; but soon, as we sit looking at the words, they shuffle, they change; and we begin saying, "Windows, yes windows—casements opening on the foam of perilous seas in faery lands forlorn." And before we know what we are doing, we have leant out of the window; we are looking for Ruth in tears amid the alien corn.

From the physical fact of the window to a Keats poem to the Bible: leaps of intuition and association without causal links. Or, she continues, take the sign "Passing Russell Square"; repeat the words like mantras and their "sunken meanings" surface:

> The word "passing" suggested the transience of things, the
> passing of time and the changes of human life. Then the word
> "Russell" suggested the rustling of leaves and the skirt on
> the polished floor; also the ducal house of Bedford and half
> the history of England. Finally the word "Square" brings
> in the sight, the shape of an actual square combined with
> some visual suggestion of the stark angularity of stucco. Thus
> one sentence of the simplest kind rouses the imagination, the
> memory, the eye and the ear—all combine in reading it.

And so it is with Woolf's own writing, which corresponds precisely to her description of the nature of words. They have, she says, a "need of change . . . because the truth they try to catch is many-sided, and they convey it by being themselves many-sided, flashing this way, then that."

In the loose but finely controlled style of which Woolf is a master, the words can flash in and out of time frames and even flash from speaker to speaker as one consciousness gives way to another, without warning or editorial direction. This is what is usually called stream of consciousness, a term often used to describe Woolf's prose. Here is an account of it by the great critic Erich Auerbach. Woolf, he observes, attempts "to render the flow and the play of consciousness adrift in the current of changing impressions" (*Mimesis*, 1946). She has reversed the usual relationship between interior events and narrative events, where the former has always been subordinate to the latter and where inner thoughts comment on or prepare the ground for the movement of plot. But, "in Virginia Woolf's case," Auerbach explains, "the external events have lost their hegemony, they serve to release and interpret inner events."

Here, for example, is Mrs. Dalloway, walking toward Bond Street in London and thinking about her inevitable demise:

> *Did it matter then, she asked herself, did it matter that*
> *she must inevitably cease completely; all this must go*
> *on without her; did she resent it; or did it not become*
> *consoling to believe that death ended absolutely? but that*
> *somehow in the streets of London, on the ebb and flow of*
> *things, here, there, she survived, Peter survived, lived in*
> *each other, she being part, she was positive, of the trees at*
> *home; of the house there, ugly, rambling all to bits and*
> *pieces as it was; part of people she had never met; being*
> *laid out like a mist between the people she knew best, who*
> *lifted her on their branches as she had seen the trees lift*
> *the mist, but it spread ever so far, her life, herself.*
>
> (1925)

Is this a sentence? It doesn't have a beginning, middle, or end, and as you read it you can't chart its progress toward a designed close. Who says "she was positive"? Is it Mrs. Dalloway, declaring her certainty to herself? Is it Woolf, standing outside her character and pronouncing authoritatively on Mrs.

Dalloway's inner state? The questions are unanswerable, for as Auerbach observes, "we are given not merely one person whose consciousness . . . is rendered, but many persons, with frequent"—and, I would add, unannounced—"shifts from one to the other." For a second, when "Did it matter then" is followed by "she asked herself," we seem to be in the company of a conventional narrator-novelist who reports the speech of her character. But then "did it matter" is repeated, and it is clear that what we're hearing is a musing. The perspective now ruling is an interior one; even though the third-person pronoun "she" carries the train of thought along, we sense that this is merely her form of self-reference. A sequence like "she survived, Peter survived" shows how it is done. "She survived" might be spoken by a narrator, but "Peter survived" is obviously uttered by someone who shares an intimacy with him; we cannot believe that the observation is made at a distance, by a third person, but then again, "lived in each other" seems to belong at once to Mrs. Dalloway and to her creator.

As the sentence continues, Mrs. Dalloway shares an intimacy not only with Peter but with everything—a house, trees, people, mist, branches—all of which "ebb and flow" with her and through her. Everything enters her, and she enters everything. Near its end the sentence names the action it is imitating; it spreads; she spreads, "ever so far, her life, herself." Formally, the sentence is fragmentary; no, it *is* fragments, held together barely by a soft "but," which is more like an "and," many participles, many ofs, all tumbling forward, all jumbled up, yet unified somehow by her consciousness, streaming, variegated, and always the same. An anonymous critic for the *Glasgow Herald* in 1927 got it just right: "Mrs. Woolf never for a moment becomes the detached observer of the world which she is creating; therefore her people are entirely real without ever being tangible." Inhabited, as it were, from the inside, Mrs. Dalloway receives no description of the usual novelistic kind, and yet, as a result of sentences like this one, the reader knows her better than if five paragraphs full of details and adjectives had been devoted to her.

Common sense might suggest that the loose, coordinating/non-subordinating style Woolf excels in is easier to manage than a style that requires the building of architectonic structures where words and phrases serve as foundations, stairways, bridges, basements, attics, and trusses, and the exertion and strain of control are felt at all times. But while the logic of subordination is demanding, it is also comforting precisely because of its demands. If the requirement is that every word or phrase you write must take its place in an unfolding design, that requirement is both a constraint and a guide; it gives you something to test yourself against. Have I gone off the track? Are some of my words and phrases operating in some alternative verbal universe? Are they striking off on their own, floating freely and untethered to any grammatical ground?

But that experience—of being free-floating, in flight, on the wing, not tied down—is precisely what the additive style is trying to achieve, although "achieve" may not quite be the right word, because, in the art practiced by Woolf, effects seem not to be achieved, produced after arduous labor; they just—or so is the desired impression—emerge. So if you are testing yourself against anything, it is the danger of looking as if you were trying too hard to be the kind of writer whose labors show. Although it might seem as if writing in the additive style is just a matter of putting one thing after another in no particular order (how can that be hard?), it is in fact the more difficult style to master; for the relative absence of formal constraints means that there are no rules or recipes for what to do because there are no rule or recipes for what not to do. (Remember "Nuns fret not at their convent's narrow room"; they do fine because of, not despite, being confined in a narrow space.) But that itself is a rule of a (negative) kind; don't forge bolted-down connections, don't put everything in its one and proper place, don't maintain a consistent time frame, don't sustain the integrity of the speaker's voice, don't make things clear. Before you can follow these "rules," which amount to the flouting of the decorums of hypotactic prose, you must first master those decorums; you can't depart from something with confidence unless you are fully practiced in the something you are departing from. Behind every paratactic, additive, associative sentence—even the ones written by masters like Woolf and Stein—is the subordinating, tightly designed, and controlled sentence that is *not* at the moment being written. You have to know how to write "do not lean out of the window" before you can riff on it. The answer to the question raised a while back—Are sentences written at the furthest reaches of the additive style really sentences?—is yes; they are sentences in which the logical structure of components firmly tied to one another is self-consciously relaxed. (Whew! Formalism saved again.)

How do you learn to write sentences like that? Not by trying to imitate Stein and Woolf. You need training wheels. There are writers less experimental and more conventional (in a good sense) who might serve as beginning models, not because they are un-artful or simple, but because their artfulness is (relatively) accessible and therefore available for imitation. Here is a sentence in the additive style by a truly great novelist, from what he himself considered his finest novel. The novelist is Ford Madox Ford (friend and publisher of Stein and Hemingway), and in this scene from *The Good Soldier* (1915), a man and a girl sit on a bench amid trees, unaware that a jealous woman is spying on them:

> *Anyhow, there you have the picture, the immensely tall*
> *trees, elms most of them, towering and feathering away*
> *up into the black mistiness that trees seem to gather about*
> *them at night, the silhouettes of those two upon the seat,*
> *the beams of light coming from the casino, the woman all*
> *in black peeping with fear behind the tree trunk.*

The reader is told in advance what is going to happen: the words will paint a picture, adding detail to detail. At first the picture is sketchy, even imprecise; we just see "immensely tall trees," and then the trees are given a name, but not all of them. Ford wants the scene to be more suggestive than photographic, and so the trees he gives us are less and less in focus and they recede as we look upward at their "towering." "[F]eathering away up" is a stroke of genius; it describes by making its object more indistinct and more distant. By the time it arrives, "the mistiness" attributed to the trees as something they attract and somehow produce ("the mistiness that trees seem to gather about them at night") is spreading over the entire picture; it extends to the two sitting on the bench, who are seen in silhouette because the light emanates from a distant source (from the casino). What exactly is happening? We strain to see, and our straining has its counterpart in the sentence where a woman in black—impossible to see in the mistiness—is "peeping," that is, prying and spying as we are, a stance that would seem to bear a threat until we realize that what she can't quite see is a threat to her, for she peeps "with fear."

The economy of the sentence—it packs so much in—is remarkable; the apparent ease of it is deceptive. But we can at least imitate Ford's form even if we cannot approach his achievement. Begin with a scene you might want to portray, say, a cocktail party in June, and then choose the first detail: "the agitated conversations"; which can then be filled in a bit, but just a bit: "mostly on politics"; and then comes the first present participle: "ebbing and flowing in intensity with passions surprising to those who voiced them." Now return to a static mode of description: "the music in the background incongruously soft and light"; and then put in the reader's surrogate observer: "the children listening in shadows on the staircase wondering who these people, so familiar to them as parents, uncles, doctors, and shopkeepers every day, could possibly be." Or, in sum:

*The agitated conversations, mostly on politics, ebbing and flowing in intensity with passions surprising to those who*

*voiced them, the music in the background incongruously soft
and light, the children listening in shadows on the staircase
wondering who these people, so familiar to them as parents,
uncles, doctors, and shopkeepers, could possibly be.*

As always, it is a matter of identifying the form: here a
succession of phrases strung together in the mode of apposi-
tion—each presenting itself as an equivalent of or an addition
to what precedes it—with no attempt to subordinate one to
another. As with the other exercises we have entertained, you
can do this forever, and when it comes time to do it for real—
to put this style in the service of a point you passionately want
to make or an idea you want to champion—you will be ready.

If Ford is a bit daunting, here is a sentence in the additive style from a high-level thriller, *The Likeness* (2007), by
Tana French. French's protagonist-narrator is living with four
housemates in a scene of heightened emotional intimacy. She
is summing up their life together:

*Cherry blossom falling soft on the drive, quiet smell of old
books, firelight sparkling on snow-crystalled windowpanes
at Christmastime and nothing would ever change, only the
five of us moving through this walled garden, neverending.*

Phrases powered by present participles ("falling," "sparkling," "moving") succeed one another to create the still but
moving picture this style is so good at. Halfway through, the
sentence comments explicitly on the message its form has been
delivering—"nothing would ever change"—before continu-

ing on to a final participle, "neverending," which names the impossible aspiration of both the prose and the speaker. Pretty good, and again, it can be imitated. Just imagine a scene of contentment and repose, say, sitting in a restaurant after a hard day's work, and then string together a few participial phrases: "Music playing softly in the background, the smell of steaks sizzling on the grill, waiters being attentive to our every wish"; sum up the essence of the pleasure: "and no one calling or e-mailing"; and then finish it: "only the two of us drinking in each other's eyes"; finally the word that names and extends the moment: "loving." Now play with it a little by inserting a meta-comment after "wish": "oh how I remember it"; and stick in a quick shift in tense and narrative mode: "she could almost taste it"; and, behold, you have something that is at least gesturing in the direction of Ford territory:

> Music playing softly in the background, the smell of steaks sizzling on the grill, waiters being attentive to our every wish, oh how I remember it, no one calling or e-mailing, only the two of us drinking in each other's eyes, she could almost taste it, loving.

The exercise is quite different from the one asking you to turn a three-word sentence into a hundred-word monster, but the principle is the same: have command of the repertoire of formal components and then build something out of it, and then do it again and again, until you can do it on demand. And as you work hard to acquire the skill, always keep beside you sentences produced by those who are virtuosi in the art.

# CHAPTER 7

# THE SATIRIC STYLE:
# THE RETURN OF CONTENT

OF COURSE THOSE who are virtuosi in the art aren't just doing finger exercises, practicing scales until they can play them with eyes closed. They've already done that as a preliminary to writing in the service of an intention, and that intention will be substantive, a matter of content—the intention to praise or blame or reveal or complicate or exhort or rejoice or ponder or meditate or lament or anatomize or deconstruct (pardon the word) or "justify the ways of God to Man." While formal devices are limited in number, contents are not; a book surveying or anatomizing them would go on forever (as, for example, Robert Burton's *Anatomy of Melancholy*, written over many decades, threatens to). So I'm arbitrarily going to choose one kind of content to serve as a bridge between the largely formal part of this book, the how-to-write part, and the more relaxed part, the how-to-read-and-appreciate part.

I choose satire, the art in which "human vice or folly is attacked through irony, derision or wit." That is a dictionary definition, and there are more sophisticated ones available in the literature, but it will do. It places satire somewhere between direct brutal invective and mild sarcasm. Satire is less direct than the former and more cutting than the latter. It doesn't quite come out and say what it is saying, and what it is saying is often devastating. It is a mode of writing characterized by great control of tone over the length of sentences, paragraphs, and sometimes entire volumes. Satire is obviously a content category—its content is cynicism, dyspepsia, disgust, anger—but there's a lot of formal skill in writing satire, so our training in forms will continue.

Masters of satire and satiric wit write sentences that deliver their sting in stages; just when the reader thinks he knows what point has been made and at whose expense, the thing opens up to claim its victim or victims more intensely. Here is an example from J. L. Austin's *How to Do Things with Words* (1962). Austin is cautioning readers not to be impatient with the slow unfolding of his argument:

> *And we must at all costs avoid over-simplification, which one might be tempted to call the occupational disease of philosophers if it were not their occupation.*

The sentence begins with a simple statement of an imperative: avoid oversimplification. The style is serious, even sober, flat. Things get more complicated in the sentence's second stage; the key is the relative clause "which one might be tempted." Suddenly the stakes are higher. Before we know what the temptation is, we know that "one" should not yield to it, and we want not to be that one. When the temptation is named—to call oversimplification the disease of philosophers—we can relax, because the spotlight has been taken away from us and turned on philosophers, who must take care not to oversimplify, a fault to which they are apparently susceptible. But then we are drawn back in by the third stage, which snaps out at both readers and philosophers. Yielding to the temptation, we learn, would be wrong not because to do so would be unkind to philosophers, but because it would not be unkind enough. The phrase "occupational disease" implies a distinction between the activity of philosophizing and a hazard that sometime accompanies it; but the word "occupation" removes the distinction; oversimplifying is what philosophers do, which means that the philosopher who is now warning us against oversimplifying is probably oversimplifying at this very moment. No one escapes the sentence unscathed.

Is there a formula here? Yes. You begin with a mild, even anodyne, statement: "It's important not to be late"; and then you add something that heightens the mood and sharpens the tone—"which is a black mark on the records of employees"—before the threat is made more explicit: "and even more so on the records of ex-employers." Not as snappy and whiplike as Austin's sentence, but in the ballpark.

The task of imitation would be harder, but certainly not

impossible, if its object were this sentence from Oscar Wilde's *The Critic as Artist* (1891). A speaker named Ernest is explaining why he dislikes memoirs:

> *They are generally written by people who have either entirely lost their memories, or have never done anything worth remembering, which, however, is, no doubt, the true explanation of their popularity, as the English public always feel perfectly at its ease when a mediocrity is talking to it.*

Memoir writers get hit twice. First they are said to be fabricators; they don't have any memories and they are just making them up. Or (and this is worse) they do have memories but what they remember is not worth reading about, is entirely without interest. And this, paradoxically, turns out to be their great value for the audience that is the sentence's real object of criticism. As the sentence makes its turn, Wilde slows down the pace so that the reader is in position to receive its final two clauses. The syntactical logic requires only the "which is"; "however" and "no doubt" are there largely to allow a pause like the moment when a roller coaster is poised at the top of its arc. To be sure, they do some work; "however" signals, somewhat unnecessarily, that the sentence's harsh judgment on memoir writing is going to be ameliorated if not reversed (in fact, it's going to get harsher); "no doubt" tells us that we should be as certain as the speaker is about the observation he will make. This certainty of conviction is conveyed also by the word "true," which nicely, and without fuss, dismisses the alternative explanations of the genre's popularity; hundreds of cultural critics are thus dispatched with a casual verbal flick. Then comes the "as" clause, which reports, apparently without emotion, the damning fact about the English public, of which Wilde's readers are presumably members. The phrase "perfectly at its ease" is perfectly deadly. On a literal level it means merely that the English public reads without undue anxiety; but this apparently neutral account of the public's posture is at the same time an indictment of its shallowness. Anything satisfies it, especially if what it reads makes no demands on an intelligence its mediocrity does not possess. What an economy of venom and disdain! (There is more economy, equal venom, but less subtlety in a sentence from Wilde's essay "The Decay of Lying" [1889] that makes a similar point: "Our splendid physique as a people is entirely due to our national stupidity.")

The trick in writing sentences like these is to open with a deadpan observation that gives no clue to the nasty turn the performance will soon take. You don't have to be an Austin or a Wilde to do it. Here is a quite nice specimen from Lee Server's biography of Ava Gardner, *Ava Gardner: "Love Is Nothing"* (2006). Server is relating the courtship (if that is the word) of the earth goddess from North Carolina by Artie Shaw, the much-married and fiercely intellectual Jewish clarinet player (their coupling was an earlier version of Arthur Miller and Marilyn Monroe). The basis of the relationship was that he talked and she listened:

> *One evening, in the middle of a discussion of the mathematics of Chopin or nuclear fusion or something, he had*

*looked at her and abruptly told her that she was in all
ways the most perfect woman he had ever met and further
that he would marry her in a minute if he hadn't already
done that too many times, which in its perfectly Shavian
way contained at the same time a boast ("Artie Shaw took
it for granted that everyone was panting to marry Artie
Shaw"), a put-down (he didn't think enough of her to
marry her), and a great compliment (he spoke as a con-
noisseur of perfect women).*

The sentence goes off its initially quiet rails with the phrase
"or something," which is at once a tribute to the breadth of
Shaw's knowledge—there were a million other things he
could have discoursed on—and a hit at his compulsion to display it. "[A]bruptly" tells its own story: Shaw doesn't bother
with any preliminaries; the shift from seminar mode to compliment (kind of) mode is instantaneous. Chopin's perfection
and Gardner's share the same category: glories Artie Shaw is
able to appreciate. He also manages, as Server observes, to
turn a confession (I've been married too many times) into a
self-advertisement. Had the sentence stopped with "times," it
would have been quite a piece of work, but Server gives it a
second act by turning the spotlight on himself and his analytical abilities. He explicates his own reporting of a moment of
which he alone seems to be the source (was he there?) and, in
a series of parenthetical interruptions that slow things down
so that we can watch him, he explicates his own explication,
lest the reader be without his authoritative direction for even
a moment. Artie Shaw has nothing on him.

Server's sentence, like Austin's and Wilde's, foregrounds the mechanics by which it launches its multidirected missiles; we are given time to see and appreciate what's happening. But a supreme sentence in the mode, written by Jonathan Swift (the English are particularly good at this), affords no such easy handles. It is, if you will pardon a very bad pun, all too swift:

> *Last week I saw a woman flayed, and you will hardly*
> *believe how much it altered her person for the worse.*

This famous sentence from the ninth section of *A Tale of a Tub* (1704) follows Swift's observation that "in most corporeal beings, which have fallen under my cognizance, the *Outside* hath been infinitely preferable to the *In*." Our sentence is offered as proof of this pronouncement. The power of the sentence comes from the disparity between its surface tone—calm, detached—and the horror beneath it. The sentence is itself an emblem of the lesson it teaches. "Last week I saw a woman" is perfectly conversational. We've all seen a woman, haven't we? That is the question the sentence proceeds to answer, first with the bombshell word "flayed," which would seem to disturb, if not destroy, the flat-footedness of "Last week I saw." But the disturbance is not registered by the speaker, who strolls right past it to express an incredulity he assumes the reader will share. By saying "*you* will hardly believe," the speaker puts his arm around the reader's shoulder and claims him as someone who sees things as he does. What they are both said to see and hardly believe is a woman whose "person" has been altered by having had her skin removed. The effect of this deadpan, clinical response to a surgical dissection depends on the ambiguity of "person," which can refer either to someone's outside (he hid it on his person) or to someone's interior qualities (what kind of person is she?). For the speaker, there is no disjunction between the two; the person *is* his or her surface, and if this is so, the removing of one surface should reveal another equally pleasing, and then another, until there remain no layers to peel off. He is surprised, and expects us to be too, when the removal of the surface—of the appearances of things—reveals something disagreeable beneath. The moral of the incident for him is the one he began with. Stay on the surface, don't look into things too closely, be content with "the Superficies," and you will be rewarded with "the sublime and refined point of felicity, called the *Possession of being well deceived*; the serene peaceful state of being a fool among knaves." This is the state into which we are invited by the sentence, and the measure of our resistance—the extent to which we recoil from the speaker's awful equanimity and refuse to become fools or knaves—is the measure of Swift's satiric success.

The form Swift deploys is fairly simple. Put together two mildly affirmed assertions, the second of which reacts to the first in a way that is absurdly inadequate: "This morning I awoke after twenty minutes of sleep and it is amazing how tired I was." "Last night I ate six whole pizzas and you would hardly believe how sick I was." "Yesterday I saw a man electrocuted and it really was surprising how quiet he became." Why are these imitations so lame, aside from the fact that

I, not Swift, wrote them? It is because nothing is at stake; their subject matter is trivial; there is nothing behind them; they are little more than a trick. Swift's sentence is certainly a trick, but it is dead serious; and behind it is a constellation of concerns about the Church, sectarian disputes, politics, education, literature, the ancients and the moderns, and much more. I know I said at the beginning of this book that it is not the thought that counts; but of course it is, ultimately. The forms on which I have placed so much (justifiable) emphasis are there for a reason they do not themselves point to; they are there for the elaboration, illumination, and powerful expression of content.

# CHAPTER 8

# FIRST SENTENCES

THIS IS OBVIOUSLY true of first sentences. If I say to you, "Go write a first sentence," you will say, "A first sentence of what?" The category of first sentence makes sense only if it is looking forward to the development of thematic concerns it perhaps only dimly foreshadows. First sentences know all about the sentences that will follow them and are in a sense last sentences (a separate category we shall get to soon). First sentences have what I call "an angle of lean"; they lean forward, inclining in the direction of the elaborations they anticipate. First sentences thus *have content in prospect*, and because they do, "first sentence" is at once a formal category and a category of substance; its members cannot stand alone, and we cannot read them, as we have read some of the sentences we have encountered, as self-contained, formal artifacts. Even the simplest first sentence is on its toes, beckoning us to the next sentence and the next and the next, promising us insights, complications, crises, and, sometimes, resolutions. There can be no formula for writing a first sentence, for the promise it holds out is unique to the imagined world it introduces, and of imagined worlds there is no end. From here on in there will be no more exercises in imitation. How can you imitate a sentence's opening out to all that lies before it?

Here is a quiet yet pregnant first sentence by Agatha Christie, the grande dame of mystery writers, known to her peers as the Queen of Crime:

> *In the afternoons it was the custom of Miss Jane Marple*
> *to unfold her second newspaper.*
>
> (*Nemesis*, 1971)

The sentence seems simple; but in fact it communicates a surprising amount of information (and more) in its brief space. Even before we meet Christie's detective-heroine, Miss Marple, we know a great deal about her. She has a routine, she follows it, and it occurs daily. Indeed, it is more than a routine. It is a custom, a word that suggests tradition, duration, and an obligatory practice tied to social and class norms. (These suggestions are enhanced by the slow progress of her full title, "Miss Jane Marple.") Moreover, one senses that "custom" is not for her a thing easily trifled with. Her customs, we intuit, are methodically, even ritualistically observed. We know this from the word "unfold"; unfolding is so much more formal than opening; merely opening a newspaper, in any which way, would seem indecorous and overhasty to her. As she unfolds it, she can take its contents in the order in which they are given, from the important news of the front page to the (to her) equally important news of the obituary page. The word that sets the seal on this mini-portrait is "second." The word is casually delivered, but because it comes late and constitutes a small surprise—it tells us that this is part two of her custom, something we hadn't been expecting—it calls attention to itself and to its message: Miss Marple is not content with one source of information; she has to know everything. And she will know everything. You wouldn't want to be someone who has something to hide.

Elmore Leonard's *Gold Coast* (1980) opens not with something hidden, but with something revealed:

> *One day Karen DeCilia put a few observations together and realized her husband Frank was sleeping with a real estate woman in Boca.*

Karen is a detective too, but we can't imagine her searching the *London Times* for information and clues; if she has "put a few observations together," it is probably by looking in pants pockets or checking the mileage of a car. The sentence that introduces Karen to us is distinguished by its speed. We aren't told what the "few observations" are or how she added them up; the "realization" comes quickly, in rapid bursts of information with no break between them (the acceleration of pace is furthered by the absence of a "that" between "realized" and "her"): husband, infidelity, woman. But not just any woman: "a real estate woman from Boca." A real estate woman is a southern Florida type often portrayed as blond, brittle, driven by avarice, a dime a dozen (this is of course a literary caricature, not a literal description). For Karen, the fact that such a woman is her husband's paramour is both infuriating and comforting; this is nothing serious and something she can take care of.

Both Christie's and Leonard's first sentences illustrate what I mean by the "angle of lean." Their sentences lean forward and point to future, if presently inchoate, vistas; they draw readers in and equip them with quite specific expectations. We know that Jane Marple will find something in her second newspaper of the day and that, whatever it is, she will follow through on it. And we know that Karen DeCilia will soon do something about what she has discovered. (What she does is figure out where her husband and the real estate woman are meeting; she then goes there and rams his Cadillac with the twin Cadillac he had bought her; a short time later, he buys two new ones; he knows the price of things.)

Our expectations are less specific after reading the first sentence of Philip Roth's *Goodbye, Columbus* (1959), but nevertheless they are strong:

> *The first time I saw Brenda she asked me to hold her glasses.*

The economy of this is marvelous. "The first time I saw" is a narrative cliché; it is often followed by something romantic, like "The first time I saw her my breath was taken away" or "The first time I saw her I couldn't stop staring." (Working against expectations is something skilled writers often do; it gives them two for one, the assertion they deliver and the one a reader may have been anticipating.) But before Neil (or the reader) knows it, Brenda has taken the sentence over and has also taken the "first time" away from the speaker, who is just someone who can perform an immediate, and minor, service. Despite having the form of a request, "she asked me" does not suggest the possibility of refusal. The fact that she has never seen him before—this is her "first time" too—doesn't matter; he's a boy of a certain age and the assumption, confirmed in the event, is that he will do anything she desires, without either question or demurrer. That is all we know, but it is enough. The relationship between the two has been set—he aspires; she lets him, as long as it pleases her—and the story can now unfold in its tragicomic arc toward the narrator's inevitable disappointment. It's all there in the first sentence.

Leonard Michaels was a contemporary of Roth's (both were born in 1933), and was often compared to him as a chronicler of Jewish anxieties. Michaels's first sentences explode off the page. Here is the opening of his short story "Honeymoon" (2000):

> One summer, at a honeymoon resort in the Catskill mountains, I saw a young woman named Sheila Kahn fall in love with her waiter.

The setup is leisurely, each detail of it setting the stage for the punch line. "One summer," in short nothing special;

" . . . at a honeymoon resort in the Catskill mountains";
yes, there are, or used to be, plenty of those; "I saw a young
woman," a honeymooner we assume, and a Jewish one by
her name. Again, all to be expected. And then the cliff the
sentence steps off: "fall in love with her waiter." That is,
the speaker saw her do something wholly at odds with her
situation—she had been married, we discover, "a few hours
earlier in the city"—saw her perform an act of social indeco-
rum; teenage girls, not just-married women, are supposed to
fall in love with waiters in the Catskills. How did it happen?
What happened next? Who is the speaker and what is his
relation to the event? How does it turn out? The sentence
propels us into the story, where we find out all this and more.

Another of Michaels's first sentences breathes menace:

> Twenty were jammed together on the stoop, tiers of heads
> made one central head, and the wings rested along the ban-
> isters, a raggedy monster of boys studying her approach.
>
> ("The Deal," 1969)

The sentence works by giving and withholding information at the same time. Twenty what? By not telling us at first,
Michaels has us waiting for a picture to be filled in, and it is,
slowly. "[O]n the stoop" locates the twenty in space but still
doesn't tell us what they are. That (small) mystery is solved by
the phrase "tiers of heads," which is more than a little maca-
bre, a suggestion of gargoyles and griffins reinforced when we
are told that the apparently disembodied heads formed one
giant head. It takes a second to realize that the wings resting

along the banisters are arms, but wings remains the image in our minds and completes the portrait of some kind of monster, which is then precisely named: "a raggedy monster of boys." The last piece—"studying her approach"—comes quickly. What lingers is the participle "studying," an action so much more threatening than "watching" or "observing." Studying means calculating as a preliminary to action, and we can only guess (with some anxiety) what that action is going to be. (It turns out to be more complicated and terrifying than anything we imagine.)

In Michaels's world, danger and threat are everywhere, and they materialize with swift force in the first sentence of "Isaac" (1969):

> *Talmudic scholar, master of Cabala, Isaac felt vulnerable to a thousand misfortunes in New York, slipped on an icy street, lay on his back, and wouldn't reach for his hat.*

Isaac's credentials are given in modifying phrases of honor ("Talmudic scholar, master of Cabala") before he is named, as if to shore him up against disaster. It is not enough. The sentence's form cannot keep back the vulnerability it immediately names. Vulnerability is not a discrete state, but an ongoing one; it travels with Isaac and asserts its power over him when he least expects it. That is why he does not fall but slips, loses his footing in a manner at once accidental and unpreventable; what can you do? His slipping does not have stages; as fast as the slight pause after a comma, he is on his back; and that's just what he expects, and because he expects it, he does nothing, not even reach for his hat, for that is going to be lost somehow, isn't it? The word "wouldn't" indicates his refusal to entertain any hope of a reprieve, however slight, from the rain of misfortune he immediately accepts. A man who believes that a bad fate can be avoided or at least ameliorated would have reached, but not Isaac. He knows.

As we can see from the examples surveyed so far, first sentences are marked by compression; they do a lot of work in a short time. ("Call me Ishmael," *Moby-Dick*; "It was love at first sight," *Catch-22*). Sometimes, as in the first sentences by Christie, Leonard, Roth, and Michaels, they perform their function of looking forward and pulling readers in by hinting at plot and character, both of which then await development. These sentences are narrative in mode; they begin to tell a story, and we want to hear the rest of it. In other first sentences the job of setting things up is done not by narrative, but by mood, metaphor, and imagery. Here is the first sentence of Nathaniel Hawthorne's *The Scarlet Letter* (1850):

> *A throng of bearded men, in sad colored garments, and grey steeple-crowned hats, intermixed with women, some wearing hoods and others bareheaded, was assembled in front of a wooden edifice, the door of which was heavily timbered with oak, and studded with iron spikes.*

There is an event here (or at least one anticipated) and human actors, but the work of the sentence is done by colors and textures arranged in a series of descriptive clauses leading to a passive action—"was assembled." The men are seen simply as beards—their faces are obscured—and as beards dressed in somber, that is, "sad" hues ("sad" also has its connotations of doleful, melancholy, desolate). These beards also wear gray pointed hats, hats that point away from the faces we do not see. There are women too, who for a moment promise to soften the scene and give it color; but they are described as hooded; we don't see their faces either. What we do see is a dark, heavy ("timbered") door that has the attributes of a weapon: "studded with iron spikes." In a scene crowded with human figures, the door is the most aggressive actor. Rather than being a portal through which one might walk, this door opens outward in a posture of threat. Its spikes are aimed at us. No one, we might think, would want to live here, and we would be right.

In Hawthorne's sentence, human actors are present, but agency is given over to somber colors and to a door. In the first sentence of D. H. Lawrence's "Tickets, Please" (1919), agency is given to a piece of machinery. Nevertheless, the sense of narrative is strong. How is this managed?

*There is in the Midlands a single-line tramway system which boldly leaves the country town and plunges off into the black, industrial countryside, up hill and down dale, through the long ugly villages of workmen's houses, over canals and railways, past churches perched high and nobly over the smoke and shadows, through stark, grimy cold little market-places, tilting away in a rush past cinemas and shops down to the hollow where the collieries are, then up again, past a little rural church, under the ash trees, on in a rush to the terminus, the last little ugly place*

*of industry, the cold little town that shivers on the edge of
the wild, gloomy country beyond.*

Here there are no human actors at all (they are presumably in the ugly villages, small houses, and picturesque
churches); there's just the tramcar, which has a personality
of its own. At first that personality is vigorous and adven-
turous; the tram moves "boldly" and it "plunges." At this
stage in the sentence, the word "black"—"black, industrial
countryside"—seems merely descriptive, but as the tram
proceeds on its way the mood begins to darken with the
first appearance of the word "ugly." The next two clauses—
"over canals and railroads, past churches perched high and
nobly"—seem to deliver a more benign landscape, until we
learn that what the churches perch over are smoke and shadows; no sunlit fields here, and the "nobility" attributed to the
churches seems more like a lofty distance from the meager
lives of the parishioners. As both the tram and the sentence
accelerate, so does the number of somber, even depressing,
words: "stark," "grimy," "cold," "ugly" "cold" again, "shivers," "gloomy." It is a feature of the sentence that words and
objects that appear early on reappear in its second half. So
we hear twice about "town" and "country" and things that
are "cold" and "little," and twice we encounter a church that
suggests (but only momentarily) a lighter and brighter vision
of things; but the tram leaves the second church behind in a
rush. What it rushes to we don't know—it is "beyond"—but
we do know that it is ugly, wild, and gloomy. And the story,
when it unfolds, bears this out.

In Lawrence's and Hawthorne's first sentences, events in the world of men and women are foreshadowed by nonhuman vehicles—tramcars, doors, colors. Although these sentences are not explicitly involved in the narration of action, they nevertheless set the stage on which action—of a human and unhappy kind—subsequently occurs. But there are first sentences where the nonhuman is not a vehicle of something else, but occupies both background and foreground. These first sentences are often meditations rather than narratives. Here is the first sentence of Ralph Waldo Emerson's "Nature" (1844):

> There are days which occur in this climate, at almost any season of the year, wherein the world reaches its perfection, when the air, the heavenly bodies, and the earth make a harmony, as if nature would indulge her offspring; when in these bleak upper sides of the planet, nothing is to desire that we have heard of the happiest latitudes, and we bask in the shining hours of Florida and Cuba; when everything that has life gives sign of satisfaction and the cattle that lie on the ground seem to have great and tranquil thoughts.

The sentence is a series of "when" clauses that aren't going anywhere. They march in place, and the place is glorious. The proportion of bleakness to sunlight is the reverse of what it is in Lawrence's sentence. The "bleak upper sides of the planet" are mentioned only to be dispelled and sent away. Indeed, it is the business of the sentence to transform time-bound particulars and variations—of emotion, thought, climate, place—into a vision of eternal bliss like the Garden of Eden or the Hesperian Gardens of Ovidian myth ("the happiest latitudes"). The first three words, "There are days," suggest that whatever these days are, they are exceptional, and unusual in "this climate." But then we are told that such days can occur "at almost any season" and we begin to suspect that it may be an inner as well as an outer weather that is being described. The hallmark of this weather is twofold: harmony among all things and the absence of thought, that is, of the kind of questioning and questing that signifies being at a distance from that harmony. When everything that lives gives sign of satisfaction, that sign is not something added to the natural repose of being; it *is* that repose, which is why the image of it is the cattle that lie on the ground, not moving, and having great and tranquil thoughts. The thoughts are great because tranquil—that is, unruffled, serene, calm, quiet, unperturbed, not really thoughts at all. Cattle, after all, don't think, which is exactly the point.

At the very opposite end of the first-sentence continuum are sentences that, rather than moving away from deliberative thought, insist on it aggressively. They are first sentences that are neither narratives nor meditations nor celebrations. They are arguments; they pose problems, issue challenges, advance theses, consider objections, draw conclusions. "Politics," the essay that follows "Nature" in Emerson's second series, is one of these:

> *In dealing with the State, we ought to remember that its*
> *institutions are not aboriginal, though they existed before*
> *we were born, that they are not superior to the citizen,*

*that every one of them was once the act of a single man,*
*every law and usage was a man's expedient to meet a*
*particular case, that they are all imitable, all alterable, we*
*may make as good, we may make better.*

This is a sentence that dismantles its putative subject. The
sentence begins by placing us in a relationship of negotiation
to the state; it is we, apparently, who must figure out how to
deal with it. The state, then, is the ostensible center of the sentence, but in fact it is its largest casualty, for it is under attack as
soon as it is named in the first clause. After that we learn only
what it is not, and with every "that" clause, the claims the state
has on us by virtue of its temporal duration are weakened. It is
not aboriginal, that is, indigenous and natural; even though its
institutions preceded us in time, they were themselves created
by single men; and they were created not in accordance with
some timeless, abstract norm, but in response to a "particular"
and, because particular, temporary need. In short the institutions that ask for our deference were made by us and "we"—
the word that takes over the sentence at its end—can remake
them or make them "better." What the sentence argues is that
faith in the state is faith in a chimera. And, moreover, faith in
law as if it were something standing above us, is a mistake, for
as Emerson says a little later, "The law is but a memorandum"
(another great sentence), the record of an agreement we may
rescind tomorrow: "The statute stands there to say, yesterday
we agreed so and so, but how feel ye this article today?" This
question is asked with an insistence difficult to ignore; that's
what the argumentative mode does.

Argumentative first sentences are not always so straight-forward. Often the argument is implicit, as it is in the first sentence of George Eliot's *Silas Marner* (1861):

> *In the days when the spinning wheels hummed busily*
> *in the farmhouses—and even great ladies, clothed in silk*
> *and thread-lace, had their toy spinning-wheels of polished*
> *oak—there might be seen, in districts far away among the*
> *lanes, or deep in the bosom of the hills, certain pallid un-*
> *dersized men who, by the side of the brawny country folk,*
> *looked like the remnants of a disinherited race.*

The sentence begins as if it were going to be an elegiac description of a bygone day ("In the days"), but it is quickly complicated and made more serious by a parenthetical observation that introduces irony, social satire, and class conflict. The leisured ladies who play at spinning with wheels that are polished toys aestheticize a genuine activity; they are the antithesis of "the brawny country folk" who do real work; they do not make the silk and lace they wear. And in the rest of the sentence a third group is introduced or half introduced. They are neither brawny nor clothed in silk. In fact they are difficult to see, small ("undersized") and so pale that they seem to emerge from some underground world "deep in the bosom of the hills." The description of them as "the remnants of a disinherited race" links them to the cursed children of Cain and the outcast wandering Jew. Who are these men? Who or what has disinherited them? What was their original sin? Can they be saved? Suddenly at the end of a sentence that began as an idealized portrait of country life we find ourselves at the beginning of a morality play and of a dissertation on class, labor, and the nature of wealth.

The morality and the argument are even more explicit in the first sentence of Booth Tarkington's *The Gentleman from Indiana* (1899):

> *There is a fertile stretch of flat lands in Indiana where unagrarian Eastern travelers, glancing from car-windows, shudder and return their eyes to interior upholstery, preferring even the swaying caparisons of a Pullman to the monotony without.*

The first part of this sentence is built on the understated (we do not notice it at first) tension between "fertile" and "unagrarian." "Fertile" is undoubtedly a positive word; it goes along with the flatness the travelers will find boring; "unagrarian" seems merely descriptive when we encounter it, as does the phrase "Eastern travelers." Things begin to sharpen with "glancing"; the Eastern travelers don't engage the fertility of the Indiana landscape; they see it out of the corners of their eyes, and they immediately recoil from it ("shudder"), from its uninteresting (to them) flatness, and turn their attention to something that is the opposite of fertility, "interior upholstery," something manufactured by turning nature's bounties into dead and meretricious—because prideful and ornamental—objects. When the sentence, in a final participial clause, makes the preference of the Eastern travelers explicit—they prefer a swaying canopy to the swaying of tall corn—we have learned to scorn their scorn. "Eastern" is now an epithet, and "un-agrarian" is now an accusation that means "incapable of appreciating or even seeing the beauties of a midwestern landscape." The final phrase, "the monotony without," is understood to be the judgment of those who look but do not see, those whose souls harbor a monotony far flatter, in a deep sense, than the fields they turn away from. The entire sentence is a judgment on them, and it pressures us to value everything they scorn.

The pressure and judgment are even greater in the first sentence of Increase Mather's *A Brief History of the War with the Indians in New-England* (1676), because its argument is presupposed and the risk of dissenting from it is made clear:

> *That the Heathen People amongst whom we live, and whose Land the Lord God of our Fathers hath given to us for a rightful Possession, have at sundry times been plotting mischievous devices against that part of the English Israel which is seated in these goings down of the Sun, no man that is an inhabitant of any considerable standing, can be ignorant.*

The argument proceeds by declaring there is no need to mount one and daring its reader to disagree on pain of being cast out. The possible objections to Mather's confident assumption of God's favor—that the land belongs to the Indians, that the English settlers are the aggressors—are disposed of briskly in a long dependent clause that, because of its "That" (such is the case) construction, forestalls disagreement. The acknowledgment that it is the settlers who live among the Indians is blunted before it is made when Mather describes the native inhabitants as "heathen people," unbelievers who because they are uncivilized and unenlightened have no rights. The phrase "whose land" gives the heathens possession for an instant, but then the syntax makes the land the object of God's having given it to someone else (The Lord giveth and the Lord taketh away), to the English Israel, to the remnant of the faithful. God's chosen move ever westward ("in these goings down of the Sun") in an effort to escape the persecution of the ungodly, but the ungodly are now encountered again in the form of the native Indians, who, like Pharaoh, vainly resist Heaven's will and hatch plots that can only come to naught. All this (and more) is assumed as an undoubted fact by the sentence's syntax. And when the independent clause finally appears, it consigns anyone who would disagree with what precedes it to the category of the ignorant, the same category to which the heathens, ignorant of the true God, themselves belong.

The form of Mather's sentence imitates the judgment of God. It is implacable. Nothing is going to stand in its way. The reader doesn't have a chance or a choice. At first glance, the opening sentence of Jeremy Taylor's *The Rule and Exercises of Holy Living* (1650) places the reader in a more independent position, but that doesn't last:

> *He that is choice of his time will also be choice of his company, and choice of his actions, lest the first engage him in vanity and loss, and the latter by being criminal, be a throwing his time and himself away, and a going back in the accounts of eternity.*

The form of the sentence is sententious; it is crisp and confident and promises to tie things down in neatly patterned parallels linked by the word "choice." But "choice" has two meanings: that which is best or prime (a choice piece of land) and the act of choosing one thing or action over another. The first meaning suggests that the scale of value is already known and obvious; the second puts pressure on the "he" who must do the choosing. Will he—will the reader—choose well? The clause sets up a triple requirement: use your time well, do what you do in the company of right-thinking companions, and perform right actions. The dependent clause (beginning with "lest") lists the dangers that await the man who fails the requirements, who wastes his time in the company of ne'er-do-wells. The dangers are parallel. Those who hook up with bad companions will be led into actions of vanity; their actions will be criminal because both time and the self will be wasted; the occasion for self-improvement will have been missed. All very neat, everything accounted for in a ledger and economy of virtue. But then the last clause, "a going back in the accounts of eternity," widens the sentence's perspective to the point where its apparent concerns are left behind. While "accounts" suggest the kind of balancing the sentence has so far been performing, the invocation of the vistas of eternity overwhelms, supersedes, and cancels all accounts. In eternity's accounts all man's choices are less than froth. Why bother? What does it matter?

To assume the perspective of eternity is to ask these questions. If in the end everything we say or do will fade into insignificance in the vast panorama of eternity, why do anything? Why write sentences? The issue is squarely joined in the first sentence of Taylor's *The Rule and Exercises of Holy Dying* (1651):

> *A man is a bubble (saith the Greek proverb); which*
> *Lucian represents with advantages and its proper circum-*
> *stances, to this purpose; saying, that all the world is a*
> *storm, and men arise up in their several generations, like*
> *bubbles descending* à Jove pluvio, *from God and the dew*
> *of heaven, from a tear and a drop of rain, from Nature and*
> *Providence: and some of these instantly sink into the deluge*
> *of their first parent, and are hidden in a sheet of water,*
> *having had no other business in the world, but to be born,*
> *that they might be able to die, others float up and down*
> *two or three turns, and suddenly disappear, and give their*
> *place to others: and they that live longest upon the face of*
> *the waters are in perpetual motion, restless and uneasy, and*
> *being crushed with the great drop of a cloud sink into flat-*
> *ness and froth; the change not being great, it being hardly*
> *possible it should be more a nothing than it was before.*

Instead of "dust unto dust," this sentence enacts (over and over again) "water unto water." There are bubbles, storms, dew, tears, rain, deluges, sheets, drops, clouds, froth—distinct names for an element that is always the same. These words are embedded in what offers itself as a narrative of the generations of man, and they have the effect of denying the distinctions the narrative is supposedly establishing, between men who die shortly after they are born, men who live for "two or three turns," and men who live long. Even these longest-lasting men live only on the face of the waters and can scarcely be said to have an identity because they are "in perpetual motion" before they sink into froth, distinguishable from those who "instantly sink into the deluge of their first parents" only by the length of the time it takes them to dissolve. Indeed, all men, however short or long lived, sink into the deluge of their parents, that is, into the original sin whose fatally and massively debilitating effects bring all men to the same abysmal level no matter what the duration of their lives or their apparent accomplishments. The sentence ostentatiously offers different forms of water, and different forms of men, and suggests (momentarily) that they are distinguishable, but in the end (and in the beginning) they are all the same, and in its final clause, the sentence openly declares what it has all the while been doing, when it tells us that the change from mortal form to water and to annihilation is no change at all, "it being hardly possible it should be more a nothing than it was before." Here is a long first sentence that tells us that there was never any place for it to go, that its forward motion is only apparent, that each moment in it is as important, or unimportant, as any other. A while back I suggested that Gertrude Stein's desire for a language that by defeating linear composition gives readers the experience of a continuous present is implicitly theological. Here is the thing itself in a first sentence that is also the last sentence and everything in between.

CHAPTER 9

# LAST SENTENCES

FIRST SENTENCES, AS we have seen, are promissory notes. Whether they foreshadow plot, sketch in character, establish mood, or jump-start arguments, the road ahead of them stretches invitingly and all things are, at least for the moment, possible. Last sentences are more constrained in their possibilities. They can sum up, refuse to sum up, change the subject, leave you satisfied, leave you wanting more, put everything into perspective, or explode perspectives. They do have one advantage: they become the heirs of the interest that is generated by everything that precedes them; they don't have to start the engine; all they have to do is shut it down. This means that they often come across as elegiac: the reader is leaving something he or she has grown fond of, and will therefore be inclined to give the benefit of the doubt to the author's parting statement. That may be the explanation for the good reputation of some last sentences that aren't really all that good, like the famous last sentence of Dickens's *A Tale of Two Cities* (1859):

> *It is a far, far better thing that I do than I have ever done before; it is a far, far better rest that I go to, than I have ever known.*

This one we could imitate forever: "It is a far, far better burger that I eat than I have ever eaten before; it is a far, far better digestive experience I go to than I have ever known." "It is a far, far better house I buy than I have ever imagined; it is a far, far better zip code I go to than I could have hoped for." The sentence is just too formulaic, mechanical, and stagey; were it not for the emotions built up in the course of the novel, no one would ever have taken note of it. (I have the same opinion of the novel's even more famous first sentence.)

Some last sentences do deserve the fame they enjoy, not because they are stand-alone achievements, but because they rise to the last-sentence occasion and do the requisite summing up. A good example is the last line of the movie *Some Like It Hot* (1959)—"Well, nobody's perfect." It is spoken by Joe E. Brown, playing a millionaire who has been courting Jerry (Jack Lemmon) in drag. Jerry has been trying to explain to Osgood (Brown's character) why they can't marry, but Osgood deflects and rebuts each reason. Finally, thinking that he has an argument Osgood cannot rebut, Jerry rips off his wig and declares, "I'm a man." The reply, "Well, no-body's perfect," entirely undoes the game of giving reasons by upending the assumptions that were supposedly driving the plot—that men and women are different, that it matters, that anything matters. Of course those assumptions were always being put into question in the movie, with its cross-dressing, reversal of gender roles, and boundary-blurring wit. It is just that "Well, nobody's perfect" reprises these (sometimes sub-terranean) themes and puts the "perfect" cap to them.

Other famous last lines do something of the same for the works they conclude. "After all, tomorrow is another day" is of course the last line of the movie *Gone With the Wind* (1939), and the last of the declarations by Scarlett O'Hara that the world will not defeat her. "Isn't it pretty to think so?" the final line of Hemingway's *The Sun Also Rises* (1926), is just as famous for its rueful and succinct expression of the novel's mixture of romanticism, cynicism, and flinty realism. ("Pretty" is the word that does most of the work; it suggests something attractive and something meretricious at the same time; it is at once an affirmative statement and a judgment on it.) "He loved Big Brother" is the celebrated last line of Or-well's *1984* (1949); in just four words it announces the dark inevitability of totalitarianism's triumph.

But these sentences will not serve my purpose here, be-cause any assessment of their impact depends on a full knowl-edge of what has preceded them. Standing alone, "Nobody's perfect" is a cliché; "Tomorrow is another day" is a banality; "Isn't it pretty to think so?" an unremarkable question; and "He loved Big Brother" an apparent piece of sentimentality.

What I'm after in this section are last sentences that yield their riches (or at least some of them) to an analysis that focuses on them in relative isolation. I say "relative" because "last sentence," like "first sentence," is both a formal and a content category. Last sentences are formal items because they can be picked out with no reference to anything that is being said; but it is only because of the things that have been said before they appear that last sentences are resonant. So in the parade of last sentences that follows, formal and thematic analysis will mix promiscuously. I shall be reading in full appreciative mode and looking for sentences that would make an impression even on those who did not know the works they bring to a close.

They needn't be long or even very serious. In the last line of the movie *The Professionals* (1966), Ralph Bellamy's character calls Lee Marvin's character a bastard. Marvin replies:

> *In my case, an accident of birth, but you, sir, you're a self-made man.*

The sentence plays on the meanings of "bastard," a person born out of wedlock and a person of bad character. "Self-made man" is usually a compliment, but here it is a sardonic and witty comment on a nominal gentleman's ability to achieve a (negative) status he wasn't born to. (The most insulting word in the sentence is "sir.")

The last line of Henry James's *The Wings of the Dove* (1902) is even shorter and decidedly serious. "We shall never be again as we were" records the realization by Kate Croy that she and Merton Densher have made for themselves a quite different future than the one they imagined they could build on Millie Theale's fragility. But you don't have to recall that to be taken by a sentence that, while short, unfolds in ever more devastating stages. "We shall" seems to predict a future, but that future is immediately taken away by "never," a word that not only bars access to a better time, but, as the construction continues, negates being itself: "We shall never be." And neither shall they ever have an "again"; time cannot flow backward and give them repeated being; they can only experience themselves as horribly different from what they were. The sentence would be an accomplishment even if we didn't know the story it brings to an end.

Ditto for the last sentence of Mary Shelley's *Frankenstein* (1818):

> *He was soon borne away by the waves and lost in darkness and distance.*

To be sure, it helps to know that "he" is the monster and that he has stepped onto an ice raft after having declaimed over the dead body of his creator. But even without that knowledge the sentence communicates the desolation and finality of his journey. There are two stages to it. Because "soon" precedes "borne away," we have a sense of rapid movement before we know what kind of movement it is; and then when we find out it is already movement "away." (Think how different it would be if the sentence read, "He was borne away by the waves soon.") Since waves are themselves movement (that's all they are), the swiftness of passage is even more heightened. "Soon" is carried over silently from the first part of the sentence and attaches itself to "lost," at once literal and the final allusion in the novel to Milton's great epic. So lost is he that his loss is described in two measures that alliterate, "darkness and distance," words that themselves have double meanings: he is dark in that he cannot be seen, and he is dark in his interior; he is distant in the literal sense of being far away and in the metaphorical sense of being apart from all other beings.

In the last sentence of Fitzgerald's *The Great Gatsby* (1925), the rhetorical effect is also carried by alliteration—a figure of speech often used to intensify emotions and assertions—but in this case the repeated consonant is *b* rather than *d*.

> *So we beat on, boats against the current, borne back cease-lessly into the past.*

The narrator, Nick Carraway, has been recalling Jay Gatsby's faith in a future that will bring him his dream: Daisy Buchanan and everything she stands for. We are all, Carraway muses, like Gatsby, running toward a promised land "that year by year recedes before us." This last sentence mimes the treadmill we are on, mocking our efforts at acceleration with a series of *b*'s—"beat," "boats," "borne," "back"—that keeps bringing us to the same place. We try to get ahead, but the current, both of life and the sentence, flows ceaselessly backward, carrying us again and again into the past, which is of course the sentence's last word. It says, here we are again.

*The Great Gatsby* is thought to have been modeled in part

on Joseph Conrad's *Heart of Darkness* (1899, 1902), also about a man who, like Gatsby, remains a mystery and seeks after meanings and values that elude him. In Conrad's novel, the metaphor of a water journey made against resistance is sustained from the opening lines to this last line:

> *The offing was barred by a black bank of clouds, and the tranquil waterway leading to the utmost ends of the earth flowed somber under an overcast sky—seemed to lead into the heart of an immense darkness.*

The phrase "barred by a black bank" might have been an alliterative pattern Fitzgerald was remembering when he wrote the last sentence of *The Great Gatsby*. Unlike Fitzgerald's sentence, Conrad's opens up and flows, but its forward movement doesn't bring us anywhere, or, rather, it brings us too far. The "offing" is a part of the sea that is distant but visible from the shore; it marks the distinction between shore and what lies beyond it, and between what is sea and what is not sea. But the first thing we learn about the offing is that we cannot see it because it is barred by black clouds; so our line of vision shifts downward to the "tranquil waterway." Normally a positive word, "tranquil" is vaguely ominous; the waterway is calm, unruffled, free from agitation, in short, empty and vast, so vast that it has no end (and therefore no beginning or middle); it flows "somber," that is, dark, gloomy, in shade (from the Latin *sub umbra*); it flows "under an overcast sky," and while "under" suggests a separation between waterway and sky, the word "overcast"—dark, obscuring—brings the two together in a gloom; and what the waterway flows into is an even vaster darkness. "Black" "clouds," "somber," "overcast," "darkness"—all words with the same connotations, and together they create the "immense darkness" waiting for us at the end of the sentence. The darkness refuses to perform as a period; it just keeps stretching on.

Both Fitzgerald's and Conrad's sentences work against the fact that sentences move in time and promise to deliver us somewhere at their conclusion. Their sentences, as we have seen, either flow backward or take us nowhere or take us to the mouth of an unfathomable immensity; they deny us the comfort that sentences, especially last sentences, normally provide, the comfort of being able to order objects and events in comprehensible patterns of cause and effect, past and present, near and far. All those distinctions—distinctions in the absence of which ordinary life could hardly be lived—are casualties of these sentences, and this is even more spectacularly the case with the last sentence of Poe's *The Narrative of Arthur Gordon Pym* (1838), where whiteness does for Poe what darkness does for Conrad. Water is again the (apparently) conveying medium. Two men in a boat are increasingly unable to see anything in front of them as a white "ashy material" covers everything. And then a huge "shrouded human figure" looms ahead, and, suddenly, the abrupt (non)end:

> And the hue of the skin of the figure was of the perfect whiteness of the snow.

"Hue" means color, and a figure is something that stands out against a ground. In the absence of a ground, a figure

could not be seen, for if it were the same as everything sur-
rounding it, it could not emerge into visibility. That is precisely the case here; the figure that looms before Pym and his
companion is indistinguishable from the background frame
that would, if it only had a hue, allow it to be picked out.
What the unhappy travelers meet in the last second of their
voyage is the end of perception. Perception requires both
distance and difference (you're one thing, I'm another), but
here there is neither. White snow, white skin, white everything. Skin is usually a covering of something, but in this
sentence, it is skin all the way down (a point made formally
by the four nested "ofs"). The skin is not only white; it is a
perfect white, a white without blemish, without seam, without beginning and end, and therefore without the capacity
to provide the reference points that make seeing "it," as opposed to anything else, possible. In some religious discourses,
this is the desired state, the undoing of perceptual distinction
in a union with divinity in which the aspirer and the object
of aspiration are indistinguishable. Identity, as a function of
difference, is no more, and the peace of God and eternity
reigns. Obviously not the case in this sentence, where the
undoing of perception and of any basis for judgment or decision is the occasion of horror, not unlike the horror Conrad's
Kurtz proclaims in *Heart of Darkness*.

Another name for the state of perceptual dissolution, the
state in which separateness and independence are no more and
we are one, as Wordsworth said, with the rocks and stones
and trees, is death, imagined either as nothing—that seems
to be Poe's imagination—or as the portal to everything. The

relationship between peace and death is what Mr. Lockwood thinks about in the last sentence of Emily Brontë's *Wuthering Heights* (1847), as he stands above the graves of Heathcliff and Catherine, who are finally at rest after lives of drama, turmoil, and pain:

> *I lingered round them, under that benign sky, watched the moths fluttering among the heath and harebells, listened to the soft wind breathing through the grass, and wondered how any one could ever imagine unquiet slumbers for the sleepers in that quiet earth.*

The four verbs that describe Lockwood's posture—"lingered," "watched," "listened," "wondered"—have the effect of stilling action and presenting a mental state that is without perturbation or movement. No straight-line motion of either body or mind, just a gentle musing that mirrors the gentle fluctuations of nature—the fluttering moths, the soft winds that breathe rather than blow, the grass that is slightly ruffled but not really disturbed, all under a calm ("benign") sky. When the sentence finally moves forward with the report of what Lockwood is wondering, it names for a second everything it has excluded—unquietness—but its point is that, at least in this moment, unquietness will not even be imagined for those who, after a lifetime of agitation, slumber. "[S]leepers in that quiet earth" puts the seal on the cessation of activity, and presents us with a sense of resolution that feels like a benediction.

Benediction is what George Eliot reads over the life of her

heroine Dorothea Brooke in the last sentence of *Middlemarch* (1900). Dorothea's "finely-touched spirit" produced benign effects in the world, but not "widely visible" ones:

> But the effect of her being on those around her was in-
> calculably diffusive: for the growing good of the world is
> partly dependent on unhistoric acts, and that things are
> not so ill with you and me as they might have been, is
> half owing to the number who lived faithfully a hidden
> life, and rest in unvisited tombs.

Eliot wrote in a Protestant tradition that privileges the interior action of faith over the performance of great deeds. The idea (Eliot would have encountered it in the poetry of Milton, especially *Paradise Regained*) is that right being—the state of a well-ordered soul—is itself an action. Dorothea's being, we are told, is the source of her effect. It is an effect that is said to be "diffusive"; that is, it spreads everywhere, a statement that at first seems hyperbolic, until it is glossed in a way that generalizes Dorothea's example to the point of universalizing it The gloss begins by assuming what it does not pause to argue for: "Good" in the world is growing, and then it attributes that good and its growth not only to Dorothea (a single attribution would have been implausible) but to all the Dorotheas of whom we necessarily know nothing. The phrase "unhistoric acts" tells it all: acts that are not played out on the world's stage, acts that are interior, acts that will go unrecorded. How could such acts be efficacious? What is their medium? The answer is that you and I are;

we are invited by the sentence to consult our own lives and then to inventory everything in them that is "not so ill," and finally to acknowledge that the good we have experienced and perhaps practice is "half owing" to those many who, although hidden from view, live "faithfully," that is, with a resolution always to be true to an internal code of values, and infect the world with a virtue that is contagious. "[H]alf owing" leaves room for individual efforts; even if the presence of a Dorothea touches and awakens us, we must still do our part, although that part may be as theatrically modest as the part she provides. And if we do our part, our reward will be as Dorothea's—to rest in "unvisited tombs," a phrase that might in some other sentence have the sound of melancholy and failure, but here rings with quiet triumph. Faithful souls need no external signs of their worth to validate them; visits would be superfluous; persons of Dorothea's "finely-touched spirit"—and oh, how wonderful to be one—need neither tombs nor visitors. They are their own monuments, as is this quietly thrilling sentence.

I do not mean to suggest that the only last sentences worth paying attention to bring either dissolution, the effacing of difference, or the "peace which passeth understanding." Some last sentences refuse both these positive and negative resolutions and keep their tensions and tumults alive till the end. Here is the last sentence of E. M. Forster's *A Passage to India* (1924). Fielding, an Englishman with "a belief in education," has just said to Dr. Aziz (they are both on horseback), "Why can't we be friends now? It's what I want. It's what you want." Aziz does not reply, but the whole world does:

> But the horses didn't want it—they swerved apart, the
> earth didn't want it, sending up rocks through which riders
> must pass single file, the temples, the tank, the jail, the
> palace, the birds, the carrion, the Guest House, that came
> into view as they issued from the gap and saw Mau be-
> neath, they didn't want it, and they said in their hundred
> voices, "No, not yet," and the sky said, "No, not there."

Nature's indifference to man is a prime trope of pasto-
ral poetry; the seasons unfold, plants and flowers live and
bloom again; the sun shines on fresh meadows, but men
and women (the words are the Greek poet Moschus's, in his
lament for Bion), "once we have died, in hollow earth we
sleep, gone down into silence, a right long and endless and
unawakening sleep." In Forster's sentence, however, nature
is an active participant in the political world and signifies
her preferences in unmistakable and myriad ways: by the
movement of the horses; by a landscape that will not allow
the two would-be friends to ride side by side (the participle
"sending up rocks" suggest that the narrow pass the rocks
create is being formed right now, in the sentence); by inanimate features of a cultural landscape that insists on its
own hegemony and will not give up anything (palaces, jails,
guesthouses); by signs (birds and carrion); and, as if these
"hundred voices" saying, "No, not yet," were insufficiently
loud and clear, by the overarching sky itself, whose voice is
even more emphatically negative: "No, not there." This is
an overdetermined no if there ever was one. The sentence
could have gone on forever and the chorus of nays would

only have been augmented, never softened. This is a last sentence that lets no one off its hook.

The peace that eludes Dr. Aziz and Fielding, the peace Dorothea has earned, the peace Cathy and Heathcliff may enjoy in their shared grave, comes to Faulkner's Benjy as the surrey he is riding in goes clip-clop at a steady pace. Here is the last sentence of *The Sound and the Fury* (1929):

> *The broken flower drooped over Ben's fist and his eyes were empty and blue and serene again as cornice and façade flowed smoothly once more from left to right, post and tree, window and doorway and signboard each in its ordered place.*

The serenity Benjy achieves depends on a regularity of sound and motion that quiets the thoughts he can't quite have. Although the sentence describes a scene of which he is the centerpiece, he, as an active consciousness, is absent from it. The drooping flower has more agency than he does. The connective "and" promises a reaction to the flower, but none comes, just the report of Benjy's empty eyes. He becomes an object in the landscape; the blueness of his eyes merging with post, tree, window, and doorway, all flowing together in a cinematic moment gloriously without content, but full of order, not the order of man's plans, but the order of things; formalism triumphant in the stilling of mind.

# CHAPTER 10

# SENTENCES THAT ARE
# ABOUT THEMSELVES
## (AREN'T THEY ALL?)

AS WE NEAR the end of our time together, let's look back and see where we've been and how far we've come. I began with a tendentious thesis: in learning how to write sentences, it is best to begin with forms and pay no attention to content. A sentence, I declared, is a structure of logical relationships; the relationships are finite and learnable; the contents that can find expression in the structures formed by the relationships are infinite and incapable of being catalogued. So it follows, I argued, that content will be a distraction and that the skill of writing well-formed, clear, and tightly organized sentences will be acquired by focusing on forms. I explained that what I meant by "forms" is not the list of parts of speech or kinds of clauses or grammatical errors found in many textbooks, but the logical forms that link actor, action, and the object of action in a way that make available simple and complicated predications. It is a matter, I said, of practice, of becoming so familiar with the tools in advance of any particular use of them that when an occasion of use turns up, you and they will be ready. I then came up with a few exercises (there are many more) that would help.

The next step was to introduce the notion of styles, arrangements of formal features designed to produce a certain effect and project a certain vision of the world. These are also innumerable, but three, I observed, are general enough to serve as teachable examples: the subordinating style, which ranks, orders, and sequences things, events, and persons in a way that strongly suggests a world where control is the imperative and everything is in its proper place; the additive style, which gives the impression of speech and writing just haphazardly tumbling out of the mouth or the thoughts of a writer who is not worrying about getting every particular just right; and the satiric style (more a thematic than a formal category), employed as a weapon by writers who want to harpoon persons, parties, or society as a whole. I illustrated these stylistic categories with sentences written by master writers who were of course trying to say something important with them, but my reading of their prose emphasized the formal resources they were deploying in ways that might be imitated by anyone willing to work at it. I hazarded some imitations myself, noting always that they were imitations of formal devices and were therefore uninteresting or even puerile in content.

And, finally, I acknowledged that in the end, content must

take center stage, for the expression of content is what writing is for; and I turned my attention to sentences that could not be regarded as stand-alone monuments, because in order to read them, never mind analyze them, it was necessary to take account of the substantive concerns that led to their being written. First and last sentences, I observed, are obvious instances; a first sentence is the preface to something, to a set of propositions or to an unfolding idea, to a meditation on the complexity of life or to a political statement (or to a thousand other things); and a last sentence is the conclusion or coda to that same something; and so to talk about first and last sentences is to talk about the role they play in a structure of content, and that is the way I have talked about them in the previous two sections. I passed from a focus on craft to a focus on meaning, from analyzing sentences to reading them. The idea was that if you know how sentences are put together in the abstract—as formal devices for delivering a nonformal payoff—you will be that much better able to engage with them, to take their measure in full, to receive what they have to give. Hence the formula "sentence craft equals sentence comprehension equals sentence appreciation."

But in reading over the pages I have written, I have become aware that they have been staging a drama or a contest between what we might call the instrumental view of language—language as the disposable vehicle of a subject matter it serves—and a view of language as a formal system that refuses to efface itself before the demands of content and instead claims generative and determining powers; meanings serve it and not the other way around; it is its own subject matter. Almost without my knowing it, the unfolding of my argument mirrored the struggle between these two views. In the opening chapters, I concentrated on language's forms, but matters of substance kept seeping in; in the later chapters, I surrendered to content, but my analyses always wanted to return to form. In this final section I will bring the two strains of the book together by looking at sentences whose content is their form—sentences self-conscious about their own composition, sentences that meditate on their own limitations, sentences that burst their limitations, sentences that invite and resist interrogation, sentences that proclaim their power, sentences that withhold their power, sentences that are great in part because they are so determinedly self-reflexive and aspire to the condition of pure objects.

First a sentence from Philip Sidney's *An Apology for Poetry* (1595) that at once tells us what a sentence can do and does it:

> *Who readeth Aeneas carrying old Anchises on his back*
> *that wisheth not it were his fortune to perform so excellent*
> *an act?*

The sentence is about the effects of reading it. The main effect is produced by the speed of the first three words. By writing "Who" instead of "He who" and by leaving out the preposition (either "of" or "about") between "readeth" and "Aeneas," Sidney delivers us to the main image of his sentence—Aeneas carrying his elderly father to Sicily after the defeat of Troy—by what feels almost like fuel injection. Usually, "readeth" would be a verb signifying distance, but the sentence rushes past the word and inserts us directly (or so it seems) into the scene. Then the sentence slows down in preparation for a reflection on the experience it has delivered. "[T]hat wisheth not it were," in contrast to what precedes it, is labored, convoluted, and indirect. The prose seems to stand between us and the wish whose negation it negates. And then it opens up again, to name that wish—"to perform so excellent an act"—a wish the reader has already realized insofar as he has been moved by the experience of reading the sentence, of performing it, to admire; and if admiration, can emulation be far behind?

The idea—the core idea of humanism—is that the act of reading about great deeds will lead you to imitate them, a sequence the young John Milton experiences when he reads Dante and Petrarch, finds himself moved by them to "more love of virtue," and comes to see that before he can presume to write of virtuous things, he must himself be virtuous:

> He who would not be frustrate of his hope to write well
> hereafter in laudable things ought himself to be a true
> Poem; that is, a composition and pattern of the best and
> honourablest things; not presuming to sing high praises of
> heroic men, or famous cities, unless he have in himself the
> experience and practice of all that which is praise-worthy.
>
> (An Apology, 1641)

This sentence, a mini-essay on the relation between ethics and aesthetics, enacts what it describes. It argues implicitly against the commonsense assumption that the craft of writing is one thing, the moral worth of the writer another. Milton insists that the two are one, and that without the latter, the former is impossible. The somewhat clotted opening of the sentence—"He who would not be"—holds us up until the sentence opens up with the word "hope" and the briskly audacious, smoothly flowing declaration that if you want to write a good poem about good things, you must yourself be the thing you write about, "a true Poem." The question raised—what exactly is a true poem?—is acknowledged by Milton when he promises, with the professorial "that is," a clarifying definition. But by the logic of his message, no definition will be sufficient, because the state of true poem-hood cannot be described from the outside. It is a feature of one's inside, and if it isn't, no amount of words will explain it. So what follows the "that is" is a series of words and phrases that are themselves in need of an explanation no discursive elaboration could possibly provide. The words "composition" and "pattern" nicely join the perspectives of writing craft and moral probity: what you can compose depends on what you are composed of. The words that follow—"best" and "honourablest"—raise the same questions as "true Poem": What exactly is the best and the most honorable? And a bit later, what is heroic? Again, the answer will be found, if it is found, "within himself"; that is where the "experience and practice of all that which is praise-worthy" reside. The objects of the sentence's high praise—heroic men, good poems, honorable deeds—never acquire explicit and visible shape in the course of its unfolding, for if they did, the sentence—itself a true poem because of its reticence—would betray itself. The sentence refuses to give up its contents.

If deeds are good and praiseworthy by virtue (literally) of the spirit from which they issue and not by virtue of the figure they cut in the world, one performs them because one must (they well up, as Milton says in the same piece, "unbidden"), and not in anticipation of the effects they may or may not produce. In 1660, on the eve of the Restoration and the dashing of his political hopes, Milton himself performs such a deed when he writes a one-hundred-page tract knowing in advance that it is likely to fall on deaf ears:

> *Thus much I should perhaps have said though I were sure I should have spoken only to trees and stones, and had none to cry to, but with the Prophet* O earth, earth, earth! *to tell the very soil itself what her perverse inhabitants are deaf to.*
>
> (The Readie and Easie Way to
> Establish a Free Commonwealth)

Behind this relatively brief sentence are echoes of at least five myths and Bible passages, with allusions to: (1) Orpheus, whose singing was so beautiful that stones hurled at him by his enemies refused to hit him; (2) Midas, whose wife or hairdresser (depending on which version you read) tried to keep secret the truth about his ass's ears by whispering it into the bulrushes only to find that the winds spread it everywhere; (3) Jason and Cadmus, each of whom, in different mythological traditions, is said to have sown dragon's teeth from which sprang up armed men whose threat was then diminished by a stone thrown into their midst; (4) Ezekiel, the hero who at God's command prophesied over a valley of dry bones as winds breathed life into them and made them into "an exceeding great army" (Ezekiel 37:10); and (5) Jeremiah 22, in which God cries, "O earth, earth, earth, hear the Word of the Lord," and warns that "if ye will not hear these words . . . this house shall be a desolation." So, in sum and in the background: a truth that will eventually be heard despite efforts to suppress it; a poet-singer who is the medium of a reviving and enlivening spirit; legions who will someday spring up; a God who punishes the wicked and rewards the righteous in his own good time, maybe (for how can we know?). The "maybe" part is represented in the sentence by an artfully placed "perhaps"—"Thus much I should perhaps have said"—an adverb that acknowledges the uncertain status of his own performance. Does he speak without concern either for the audience or for the effect his words may or may not have? Or does he even now, as what he calls the "good old cause" seems to be expiring, harbor the hope that his words will be the seeds that, when sown, will spring up into an "exceeding great army"? The hesitation conveyed by "perhaps" hangs over what follows it. "[T]hough I were sure" doesn't tell us whether he is sure or not. When he joins the Prophet in crying "earth, earth, earth," is he saying that only the earth will listen and of course it does not; or is he appropriating to himself the Spirit that speaks through Jeremiah and prophesies the destruction of his enemies? Is the deafness of earth's inhabitants dispositive? Does it signal the end of reformation's story? Or is it merely one more instance, in a very long history, of the obdurateness of those who resist God's word (as conveyed by his anointed servant, by his Orpheus) and are doomed to be cast aside when the truth they cannot hear is unmistakably revealed? The power of the sentence inheres in its refusal to resolve this basic ambiguity. It is at once relentless in its judgments and (properly) tentative about when and whether those judgments will be realized. Another sentence that knows the truth, but will not deliver it up.

The first sentence of Francis Bacon's essay "Of Truth" (1625) also hoards the truth but disguises the deed by shifting blame for it to a surrogate:

> What is Truth? *said jesting Pilate, and would not stay*
> *for an answer.*

The sentence distances itself from its content twice, first by attributing to Pilate the question it seemed to ask, and then by attributing to him the action it performs. Pilate will not stay for an answer to the posed question, but neither will the sentence, which transfers its reticence/indifference to him. The key and damning word is "jesting." Pilate has been interrogating Jesus, who has told him, "Everyone that is of the truth heareth my voice." It is then that Pilate asks, "What is truth?" (John 18:38), and immediately goes out to speak to the Jews who had brought Jesus to him. In short, he makes a philosophical quip about truth—who can know what the truth is?—and walks away, not recognizing that the Truth stands before him in the person of the man he has been asked to judge and condemn. The irony is that he will not stay for an answer he didn't even have to seek. There it is, in plain sight (like the letter in Poe's "The Purloined Letter"), in the flesh, as directly visible as you might like, but wholly invisible to darkened eyes. The joke's on him and also on any reader who expected an answer the sentence withholds.

The idea of a truth that is at once plainly accessible and wholly hidden is central to religious thought. A sentence from John Donne's *Devotions* (1624) is a veritable dissertation on it and a rhetorical tour de force to boot:

> *My God, my God, thou art a direct God, may I not say a literal God, a God that wouldst be understood literally and according to the plain sense of all thou sayest, but thou art also (Lord, I intend it to thy glory, and let no profane misinterpreter abuse it to thy diminution), thou art a figurative, a metaphorical God too, a God in whose words there is such a height of figures, such voyages, such peregrinations to fetch remote and precious metaphors, such extensions, such spreadings, such curtains of allegories, such third heavens of hyperboles, so harmonious elocutions, so retired and so reserved expressions, so commanding persuasions, so persuading commandments, such sinews even in thy milk, and such things in thy words, as all profane authors seem of the seed of the serpent that creeps, thou art the Dove that flies.*

This is, again, a sentence about itself or, to be more precise, about its inability to characterize its addressee, "My God." Its basic syntactical structure is simple: "Thou art . . ." The problem is to fill in the dots. The first part of the sentence tells us that there is no problem at all, for the object to be known and described is "direct," "literal," and "plain," words implying that little in the way of interpretation is required. Not only does this God mean what he says, but what he says can be "understood literally," that is, with no reaching after a meaning that is perfectly present. But God's literalism—the instantaneous conveyance of his intentions—is a feature of eternity where those to whom he speaks dwell within him; he is always, in a sense, speaking to himself; there is no distance to be bridged; no translation, in the root sense of being carried across space, is necessary. Mortal men and women, in contrast, live at a distance from one another—that's why they have to write sentences—and at an even greater distance from a realm to which they have no access. Their perspective is limited by time and space, and because the discursive structures they employ reflect that limitation, the literalism they can achieve—the literalism of the here and now—is spectacularly inadequate to the literalism Donne celebrates as God's. That is why his sentence does not end with the proclamation of God's "plain sense"; the real question is how do we get even a glimpse of that plainness when the instruments (of cognition, understanding, human language, sentences) at our disposal are actually obstructions, are in the way?

The answer is to refuse the confines of the medium and deploy it as a springboard to truths it cannot express; use mortal language while bending, stretching, and even breaking it at the same time. That is what Donne does after the turn in his sentence "but thou art also . . ." But before he continues, he parenthetically warns away the "profane misinterpreter," who might mistake his intention (a danger that increases as earthly literalism is left behind). A profane mis-interpreter is a secular interpreter, an interpreter who because he is not spiritual is literal in the wrong way. Donne knows that no mere imprecation can protect him from those who do not have within them that which moves him to write. He just has to clear the decks before he flies.

And fly he does as he at once characterizes and performs the language in which God speaks. It is a language that is always pointing away from itself to something that transcends it, something that is, literally, out of this world. It is figura-tive, that is, always departing from ordinary meaning. It is metaphorical, that is, rubbing two literalisms together so as to produce something never imagined before. And once its flight pattern is established, the language soars higher, moving not only into allegories (double-sided discourse) but "curtained," obscured allegories; not only into figures, but heights of fig-ures, figures of figures; not only into hyperboles, but third-heaven hyperboles, hyperboles that reside where God lives, where what is said is "unspeakable" (2 Corinthians 12:4) be-cause it does not have to be spoken. Just before its end, the sentence descends to earth and to the literalism it strives to leave behind—"the seed of the serpent that creeps"—before it rises again with the final completion of the "Thou art" pat-tern: "thou art the Dove that flies," which means, impossibly, that Jesus is simultaneously the one baptized by John in the river Jordan and the Dove that descends from above (that is, from himself) to confirm the baptism and his identity as God. Quite a trick, and while Donne's sentence does not, could not, match it, it gets as close as we are likely ever to get in merely mortal prose.

The extraordinary power of language to communicate a reality its forms cannot present is not limited to instances of religious yearning. It is both the accomplishment and often the explicit subject of those who profess the religion of Art. Here are two sentences by worshipper Joseph Conrad.

The first is from the preface to *The Nigger of the "Narcissus"* (1897), which begins by declaring, "A work that aspires, however humbly, to the condition of art should carry its justification in every line." A few sentences later, Conrad elaborates:

> *And it is only through complete, unswerving devotion*
> *to the perfect blending of form and substance; it is only*
> *through an unremitting, never discouraged care for the*
> *shape and ring of sentences that an approach can be made*
> *to plasticity, to colour, and the light of magic suggestive-*
> *ness may be brought to play for an evanescent instant over*
> *the commonplace surfaces of words, of the old, old words,*
> *worn thin, defaced by ages of careless usage.*

The first part of the sentence names the requirements—complete devotion, perfect blending, unremitting care—phrases that seem preliminary to a celebration of art's ineffable power, but in fact turn out to be preliminary to a celebration of sentences, of their "shape and ring." "Shape" suggests something firm and crisp, something self-contained; but (another surprise) the firmness is valued as a way to something decidedly not firm, to "plasticity," an availability to being molded and remolded. The shape of an artfully made sentence, like a piece of sculpture, can be turned this way and that, revealing from each new perspective new meanings, new shades, new colors; and in that way it can become the vehicle of a "magic suggestiveness," magic because nothing in the mere surface form—the form that might be grammatically parsed—hints of it.

As Conrad's sentence proceeds, it moves into the very realm of the suggestiveness it invokes while refusing, as it must, to arrest it; it is glimpsed, here and in the sentences of other artists, only in an instant, and that instant is "evanescent"—that is, transitory, fleeting, capable of being intermittently experienced, but not of being captured and pinned down. The miracle, and the magic, is that such moments of evanescence can be produced by language that in its mundane uses sits inert on the page. The phrase "evanescent instant" is poised between "play" and its adverb "over," which then deposits us on "the commonplace surfaces of words." The evanescent instant has occurred in the space between the action and its usual commonplace result, has occurred, as it were, in the syntax; but it can be sustained for a microsecond only, and the sentence ends with an almost elegiac caressing of the threadbare material out of which the marvelous can sometimes be made: "old, old words, worn thin, defaced by ages of careless usage." The barely submerged image is of a coin, a piece of currency, exchanged and made use of many times until it has almost been worn away and seems incapable of regaining a pristine value. Except in sentences like this one where there is no careless usage at all, and more than a hint of the evanescent instant that makes language, at least for a microsecond, magical.

Two years later, in *Heart of Darkness*, Conrad's aesthetic reappears as a description of Marlow's tale-telling:

> *The yarns of seamen have a direct simplicity, the whole*
> *meaning of which lies within the shell of a cracked nut,*
> *but Marlow was not typical (if his propensity to spin*
> *yarns be excepted), and to him the meaning of an episode*
> *was not inside like a kernel but outside, enveloping the*
> *tale which brought it out only as a glow brings out a haze,*
> *in the likeness of one of these misty halos that sometimes*
> *are made visible by the spectral illumination of moonshine.*

The sentence's independent clause is as directly simple as the yarns it reports; its meaning, like the meaning seamen deliver, is easily extracted. But when Marlow's atypicality becomes the sentence's subject, meaning become elusive and is ever receding. First we learn that in Marlow's yarns, meaning, rather than being a kernel wrapped inside the prose, is on the outside. But what does it mean for meaning to be on the outside? The successive clauses that labor to tell us only deepen the question. Look at the "it" in "enveloping the tale which brought it out." "It" is the meaning that is brought out by a tale enveloped—everywhere surrounded and enwrapped—by, guess what, the meaning; the meaning is its own membrane. But that's not quite it, because it is too visually specific; hence the qualification "only as a glow brings out a haze." A glow is a light produced by something else; it is a second-order phenomenon. A haze, an opaque vapor, is the effect of a glow; it is even more insubstantial, a third-order phenomenon. But that's not quite it either. It—the meaning, the glow, the haze—should be understood not as itself but like something ("in the likeness"), like a misty halo, a cloudy luminescence, a light that is dim and barely seen; you can't be sure you see it, because its illumination (a word that names what the sentence withholds) is spectral, ghostly, and a form of moonshine, that is, of talk that is either visionary or foolish. Which is it? The sentence doesn't tell us, and we leave it not quite knowing of what kind of moonshine it itself is made or what meaning really is.

Conrad was (for a time) a friend and collaborator of Ford Madox Ford's. Ford admired Conrad's writing and, in his 1911 essay "The Critical Attitude," paired him with Henry James. The two were united, he said, by "an extreme literary conscientiousness"; that is, both cared only for their art. The compliment could be extended to Ford himself, who wrote in the preface to the 1927 edition of *The Good Soldier* (a novel nearly every sentence of which merits a place in this book), "I have always been mad about writing—about the way writing should be done." The madness, in several senses, is shared by the novel's narrator, John Dowell, who pauses frequently to reflect on the act of writing. In fact the construction of the story is his obsession, as we can tell from the famous first sentence:

*This is the saddest story I have ever heard.*

The irony is that Dowell is incapable of understanding the story he tells, incapable of plumbing its true sadness, because there is nothing inside him, no human investment in relation to which the things he experiences can be made sense of. *That* is the saddest story, the story of what he can neither see nor feel. He says of himself, "No one is interested in me, for I have no interests" (a marvelous sentence in itself). He is fixated on the act of composition because he thinks if he puts things down correctly the meaning he hasn't got a clue about will emerge. In his eyes, the problem he faces is merely a technical one:

> *I don't know how it is best to put this thing down—*
> *whether it would be better to try and tell the story from*
> *the beginning, as if it were a story; or whether to tell it*
> *from this distance of time, as it reached me from the lips of*
> *Leonora or from those of Edward himself.*

The question, which he cannot really even approach, is what kind of "thing" this is. To him the story—of multiple betrayals, destructive passions, casual cruelties, monstrous sentimentalities—is simply a problem in composition; the "better" he seeks is the better order. (He is Faulkner's Benjy, but under the misapprehension that he has a functioning brain.) The alternatives he considers—telling the story in an immediate present "from the beginning" or filtering it through the words of others and through the lens of time—are textbook alternatives from primers on how to construct a narrative. What "reaches" him are verbal and painterly memories of which he can make no final sense. And he knows it, knows that even after all is revealed, he remains uncomprehending, but he cannot even comprehend his incomprehension:

> *But the inconvenient—well, hang it all, I will say it—the damnable nuisance of the whole thing is, that with all the taking for granted, you never really get an inch deeper than the things I have catalogued.*

This sentence is an example of Ford's ability fully to present a character and allow us to see through him at the same time. "Inconvenient" is a word that marks Dowell's deepest emotional level. When he announces that he will discard the politeness of the circumlocution and say something more raw and real, all he can come up with is "damnable nuisance," a class-bound epithet even more conventional and empty than "inconvenient." And what is the nuisance? Well, no matter how much he recalls and catalogues, he can never get beneath the surface. For him, never getting beneath the surface is the equivalent of not being able to get into a room or having to wait until a door is opened. It's just a nuisance, not the occasion for a deep insight of the kind Conrad's Kurtz has when he cries, "the horror, the horror." Ford's Dowell is as incapable of saying anything like that as he is of feeling more than annoyed or inconvenienced.

Still, the cataloguing of life's details even by an unseeing person can generate great sentences that reveal much the cataloguer cannot see.

*Whole castles have vanished from my memory, whole
cities that I have never visited again, but that white room,
festooned with papier-mâché fruits and flowers; the tall
windows; the many tables; the black screen round the door
with three golden cranes flying upward on each panel;
the palm tree in the centre of the room; the swish of the
waiter's feet; the cold expensive elegance; the mien of the
diners as they came in every evening—their air of earnest-
ness as if they must go through a meal prescribed by the
Kur authorities and their air of sobriety as if they must
seek not by any means to enjoy their meals—those things
I shall not easily forget.*

The room comes alive in its deadness; its whiteness functions as a blank screen, which is then filled in by a succession
of precisely realized details (it's like painting by numbers),
details that are resolutely inanimate even when human beings
are brought in. Not fruits and flowers, but papier-mâché fruits
and flowers; cranes that are golden against a background of
black lacquer; waiters' feet, which are as much objects as the
tables (one doesn't actually look at waiters, does one?); the appearance ("mien") of the diners, who are nothing but appearance and who "go through" their prescribed forms without
ever allowing them to spill over into emotions (like pleasure)
they do not have. And the narrator? The clauses piled up and
chock full of precise observations create a pressure for, and an
expectation of, a response to the inertly busy canvas they fill
out. But the response we get—"those things I shall not easily
forget"—is underwhelming, anticlimactic, even bathetic. He

won't forget these things, but what does he think of them? Does he think anything of them at all?

Dowell finally solves his compositional problem by deciding to stop worrying about it and just tell the story as it occurs to him. The announcement of his intention to do so produces a sentence of great, and entirely impersonal, beauty:

> And I shall go on talking, in a low voice while the sea sounds in the distance and overhead the great black flood of wind polishes the bright stars.

The low voice Dowell will speak in becomes lower and even inaudible as the *s* (or soft *c*) of "voice" is quite literally absorbed by "sea sounds in the distance." "Sounds" is a verb here, but its noun sense is strongly felt: "voice," "sea," "sounds," "distance"; as the words succeed one another, the muted murmuring of a human voice becomes indistinguishable from nature's rhythms. In the second half of the sentence the now impersonal voice finds its impersonal audience in the wind and the stars. While the word "flood" is used metaphorically to describe the wind, its nonmetaphorical meaning reaches back to the sea and its sounds. Sea, wind, stars—all meld into a cosmic conversation in which there are no propositions, only sounds. The wind that polishes the bright stars is the representative in the sentence of the stylist (Ford sensed behind Dowell) who polishes the language until it shines with the diamond-like hardness the sentence displays; it has become an object.

Much later Dowell apologizes for telling his story "in a

very rambling way": "One remembers points that one has forgotten and one explains them all the more minutely since one recognizes that one has forgotten to mention them in their proper places . . ." Characters, incidents, episodes, moments appear and then appear again in a manner that seems haphazard but is really designed, if not by Dowell then by Ford, and if not by Ford then by life itself. In his masterpiece, *A Dance to the Music of Time* (1951–1975), Anthony Powell presides over not one but twelve novels in which characters, motifs, and concerns move in and out in what might be a bewildering array were it not for the control the author exerts; and it is all laid out in a master sentence at the very beginning. Powell's narrator, Nick Jenkins, has been thinking about Nicolas Poussin's great painting *Dance to the Music of Time* (1640), "in which the Seasons, hand in hand and facing outward, tread in rhythm to the notes of the lyre that the winged and naked greybeard plays":

> The image of Time brought thoughts of mortality, of human beings, facing outwards like the Seasons, moving hand in hand in intricate measure, stepping slowly, methodically, sometimes a trifle awkwardly, in evolutions that take recognisable shape, or breaking into seemingly meaningless gyrations, while partners disappear only to reappear again, once more giving pattern to the spectacle, unable to control the melody, unable, perhaps, to control the dance.

The image of time provokes Jenkins to thoughts of mortality and human beings, because only mortal beings experience time as a shaping medium, which means that only mortal beings write, or need to write, sentences. Mortality is the condition of being able to die, regarded by many as a curse, but more properly appreciated as a gift, the gift of design and choice, of gain and loss, of hope and desperation, of failure and redemption, all modes of being that are available only to creatures who, like sentences (and novels), have a beginning, a middle, and an end. It is the inevitability and shadow of death that provides life with a narrative arc, and provides moments in that narrative with a meaning; for the meaning of a moment—its distinctiveness—is a function of the place prepared for it by a past and the place waiting for it in a future that has (again, like a sentence) a terminal point. We say to ourselves, "Yes, this is where it was all leading" or "This is the beginning of something that will, I hope, flower." Without the specter and period of death, there would be no urgency of accomplishment, no expectations to be realized or disappointed, no anxieties to be allayed. Each moment would bear an equal weight or equal weight-lessness, the ideal, you will remember, to which Gertrude Stein aspired. Significance would not be in the process of emerging, sometimes clear, sometimes not; rather, it would be evenly distributed and therefore not be significance—a concept that requires that some moments stand out—at all. In short, there would be no sentences, no temporal ordering of events in an attempt to make sense of them and of life. The meaning of things would be immediately and transparently present and it would be everywhere and always the same. This is the condition of eternity, a state of being we mortals can know only by negative inference, by imagining, in time, the negation of time, as Donne does in this magnificent sentence:

> *Eternity is not an everlasting flux of time, but time is a short parenthesis in a long period, and eternity had been the same as it is, though time had never been.*
>
> (*Devotions*)

Time is an artificial breach in eternity (Donne calls it "this imaginary half-nothing"), an imperfection that springs from the nature of an imperfect, finite, transitory creature. The same imperfection and finitude require from us the writing of sentences (as opposed to the instantaneous knowledge of everything), and some of those sentences, like this one of Nick Jenkins's, reflect self-consciously on the conditions of their performance. Jenkins imagines human beings, mortal men and women, moving through the narratives of their lives in uncertain, halting, yet purposeful rhythms, which are also the rhythms of his sentence. At first the partners in this dance participate in an intricate measure, a phrase that suggests order and control. But then the measure, while methodical, slows down, loses some of its precision and becomes awkward; it begins to evolve, that is, change in ways of which those living out the change may be unaware. Still, there remain "recognizable shapes," at least for an instant, before some of them become meaningless as connections ("partners") disappear and patterns are lost. But not forever; patterns reemerge, partners reconnect, the dance continues; the melody, which sets the pace and guides the steps, can still be heard, but just who or what controls it is not clear. Yet despite all this faltering and hesitancy, meanings do develop, and even, as the next sentence says, "become in due course uncompromisingly clear," at least in the evanescent instances Conrad bows before and every committed stylist of sentences prays for.

The tension (a weak word) between the temporality of sentences and the eternity that would render them and the strivings they portray superfluous is powerfully captured in my final example, a sentence from Bunyan's *The Pilgrim's Progress* (1678). Although I have read and taught this sentence hundreds of times, it never fails to knock my socks off. Bunyan's hero, Christian, has become aware that there is a burden (original sin) on his back and he will do anything to rid himself of it. He is told that he must fly from the "wrath to come"—that is, from eternal damnation—and in response he begins to run:

> *Now he had not run far from his own door, but his wife*
> *and children perceiving it, began crying after him to*
> *return, but the man put his fingers in his ears, and ran*
> *on, crying, Life! life! eternal life.*

The sentence is about two levels of "perceiving," two kinds of crying, and two kinds of lives. Christian's wife and children perceive the head of their household abandoning them. The obligations he pushes away with a "but" (you can feel it) are great; that is why he puts his fingers in his ears. But the pull of what he runs toward is even stronger, even though he does not yet see where it is to be found. (He just runs, we have been told, "towards the middle of the plain.") His family's crying has its source in all the human ties that bind; his crying has its source in Eternity's severe requirements and the reward it holds out, however obscurely, to those who are faithful to them: "Life! life! eternal life." The sentence names the reward, but cannot bestow it; it can, however, make us feel both its inestimable price and the price we, as mortal sentence makers, time-bound creatures, are asked to pay. And given a choice between eternity and some of the sentences we have lingered over together, who knows?

# EPILOGUE

OF COURSE THERE are more sentences to celebrate and many more authors to praise. The list of writers who didn't but could have made it into these pages is considerably larger than the list of writers who did. My hope is that this discussion will be continued, and I invite those readers who can't believe I failed to include their all-time favorite sentence to send it to me; perhaps there will be a second edition. Meanwhile, there is much to enjoy; there are many sentences to read, to take apart, to caress, and to write. As I said when we began, sentence craft and sentence appreciation are not trivial pursuits. They engage us in the stringent and salutary exploration of the linguistic resources out of which our lives and our very selves are made. As usual, Gertrude Stein said it best:

> *I really do not know that anything has ever been more exciting than diagramming sentences. I suppose other things may be more exciting to others when they are at school but to me undoubtedly when I was at school the really completely exciting thing was diagramming sentences and that has ever been to me since the one thing that has been completely exciting and completely completing. I like the feeling the everlasting feeling of sentences as they diagram themselves. In that way one is completely possessing something and incidentally one's self.*
>
> (*Lectures in America*)

When Stein says that she likes "the everlasting feeling," it seems for an instant that what she likes is something she, as an active agent, is doing. But as her sentence continues, we discover that the feeling she likes belongs to the sentences she is diagramming, and that, moreover, they are diagramming themselves. She is just along for the (rigorous and demanding) ride. The reason diagramming sentences is completing is because the completing is being performed by the sentences themselves; they do it; all we have to do is attend. And if we attend faithfully, surrendering to the unfolding logic of predication, not only the completing, but the excitement of its having been done, will be ours by proxy. The reward for the effacing of ourselves before the altar of sentences will be that "incidentally" (what a great word!)—without looking for it—we will possess a better self than the self we would have possessed had we not put ourselves in service. Sentences can save us. Who could ask for anything more?

# ACKNOWLEDGMENTS

I AM FIRST of all grateful to HarperCollins editor Julia Cheif-fetz, whose idea this book was. She also gave it its title. My wife, Jane Tompkins, provided the subtitle. The book took shape as the result of extensive conversations with Julia; she told me what she had in mind and I tried to come up with it. A first draft didn't quite work and Julia and I had another long talk. At the same time I asked my wife and my friends Jerry Graff and Cathy Birkenstein to help. They read the manuscript and told me what was wrong. I followed every suggestion they made and produced the version you have in your hand. It is customary to say that Julia, Jane, Jerry, and Cathy bear no responsibility for the finished book, but they do. An incredibly careful and talented copyeditor smoothed out many of the rough spots and caught enough errors of citation to embarrass me. Throughout all of this, my agent, Melissa Flashman, kept track of everything and functioned as an honest broker. It doesn't take a village, but it certainly takes friends.

# INDEX

*Index*

# ABOUT THE AUTHOR

STANLEY FISH IS the Davidson-Kahn Distinguished University Professor and a professor of law at Florida International University. He has previously taught at the University of California at Berkeley, Johns Hopkins University, Duke University, and the University of Illinois at Chicago, where he was dean of the College of Liberal Arts and Sciences. He has received many honors and awards, including being named the Chicagoan of the Year for Culture. He is the author of twelve books and is now a weekly online columnist for the *New York Times*. He resides in Andes, NY; New York City; and Delray Beach, Florida; with his wife, Jane Tompkins.